Persian Mythology

DON NARDO

LUCENT BOOKS

A part of Gale, Cengage Learning

GALE
CENGAGE Learning·

Detroit • New York • San Francisco • New Haven, Conn • Waterville, Maine • London

© 2013 Gale, Cengage Learning

LIBRARY OF CONGRESS CATALOGING-IN-PUBLICATION DATA

Nardo, Don, 1947-
 Persian mythology / by Don Nardo.
   p. cm. -- (Mythology and culture worldwide)
 Includes bibliographical references and index.
 ISBN 978-1-4205-0794-2
 1. Mythology, Iranian--Juvenile literature. I. Title.
 BL2270.N37 2013
 299'.15--dc23
                                                    2012022862

Lucent Books
27500 Drake Rd.
Farmington Hills, MI 48331

ISBN-13: 978-1-4205-0794-2
ISBN-10: 1-4205-0794-X

Printed in the United States of America
1 2 3 4 5 6 7 16 15 14 13 12

TABLE OF CONTENTS

Map of Ancient Persia

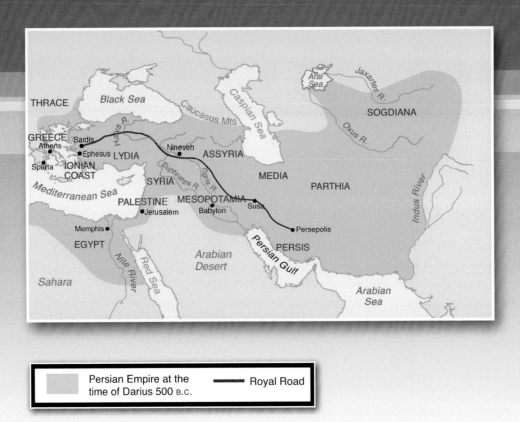

Character Groupings in Persian Mythology

Traditional Gods

Anahita Verethragna

Mithra Tishtrya

Ahura-Mazda

The One True God

Ahura-Mazda

Mythical Human Kings

Yima

Gayo-maretan

Hushang

Kay Kavus

Shahrivar

Force of Evil

Angra-Mainyu

Demons

Apaosha

Azhi Dahaka

Div-e-sipid

Mythical Heroes

Yima

Thraetaona

Zal

Rustam

Real Human Kings

Cyrus II

Cambyses

Darius I

Darius II

Alexander the Great

Ardashir II

The Prophet

Zoroaster

Major Characters in Persian Mythology

Character Name	Pronunciation	Description
Ahura-Mazda	(a-HOO-ruh-MAZ-duh)	In ancient Persia, at first a sky god and later, in the religion of Zoroaster, the one true god.
Alexander the Great		The Macedonian Greek king who conquered the Persian Empire in the late fourth century B.C.
Anahita	(ah-nuh-HEE-tuh)	The Persian goddess of the waters.
Angra-Mainyu (or Ahriman)	(ANG-ruh-MUN-yoo) or (AR-ee-mohn)	The devil-like evil force or being who opposed Ahura-Mazda.
Apaosha	(ah-pah-OH-shuh)	A demon who inflicted drought on humankind.
Amesha Spenta	(uh-MESH-uh-SPEN-tuh)	The archangels (leading angels) of Ahura-Mazda.
Astyages	(uh-STEE-uh-jeez)	King of the Medes, who was defeated by Cyrus II.
Atar	(uh-DAR)	A mythical being or force that personified fire.
Azhi Dahaka	(AH-zee-duh-HAH-kah)	One of the leading demons that did Angra-Mainyu's dirty work.
Cyrus II	(SY-rus)	The king who established the Persian empire in the 500s B.C.
Darius I	(DAIR-ee-us or duh-RY-us)	The third king of the Persian Empire.
Hushang	(HOO-shang)	The mythical early Persian king who was frequently plagued by demons.
Kay Kavus	(ky-KAH-voos)	A mythical early Persian king who discovered how to make fire.
Mithra (or Mithras)	(MITH-ruh) or (MITH-rus)	The Persian god of the sun.

Rustam (or Rostam)	**(roos-TAM) or (ros-TAM)**	The greatest of the mythical Persian heroes, who slew several evil creatures, including the infamous White Demon.
Scheherazade	**(sh'hair-uh-ZAHD)**	In the so-called *Arabian Nights,* a princess who told a story every night for a thousand nights.
Soshyant	**(SAW-shee-int)**	The third and last savior of the world, who, according to Zoroastrian beliefs, will appear in the future.
Tahmures	**(tah-MOOR-us)**	A mythical early Persian king who helped the human race acquire writing skills.
Thraetaona	**(tri-TAH-nuh)**	An early mythical Persian hero known for killing monsters and demons.
Tishtrya	**(tish-TREE-uh)**	The ancient Persian god of rain.
Verethragna	**(vair-uh-THRAG-nuh)**	The early Persian god or force of victory, often viewed as a war god.
Vishtaspa	**(VISH-tas-pah)**	A king of a land in central Asia who became the first convert to the faith preached by Zoroaster.
Vohu Manah	**(VOH-uh-MAH-na)**	One of the most important of the archangels, he brought Zoroaster to meet Ahura-Mazda.
Yima	**(YEE-mah)**	A mythical early Persian king who saved humanity from destruction.
Zoroaster (or Zarathustra)	**(ZOR-oh-ass-ter) or (zair-uh-THOOS-truh)**	The human prophet who was selected by Ahura-Mazda to preach the one true religion to humankind.

Why Persian Myths Remain Relevant

The myths of the ancient Persians reflect their customs and institutions, as well as deep-seated aspects of the Persian character. The Persians were an ambitious, highly successful people whose culture first arose in the 800s and 700s B.C., in what is now southern Iran. Like other peoples around the world, these early Persians had a number of myths connected to their own local culture.

In the mid-500s B.C. a Persian prince named Cyrus established an empire that eventually covered all of the Middle East and beyond. As a result, for more than two centuries the Persian kings ruled not only their own people, but also a vast assemblage of non-Persian peoples. Over time some of the myths and folktales of those peoples were absorbed by the Persians. This first Persian Empire fell to the Greeks in the 330s and 320s B.C. But a few centuries later, a second large Persian realm, the Sassanian Empire, took control of major portions of the Middle East. The Sassanians eagerly and almost reverently restored older Persian customs, literature, and myths.

Influence and Survival of Persian Myths

Both the early and later Persians developed mythical events and figures to explain their physical setting, their religious beliefs and rituals, political and social customs, and many other aspects of their lives. Those tales are part of the rich stream of old Persian religious and cultural ideas kept alive in Iran today. The main reason for this continued existence of ancient beliefs and customs is that the religion practiced by members of Persia's upper classes (and maybe some members of its lower classes)—Zoroastrianism—did not die out, as so many other ancient faiths did. Instead, the ancient Persian faith survived and is still practiced today. Though most modern Iranians are Muslim, a small minority of the population remains Zoroastrian.

That religious survival has been strengthened by a parallel development. In the mid-twentieth century, several Iranian political leaders urged their people to forge a cultural link with their glorious past. It became fashionable for Iranians to think of themselves as Persians and to speak of the accomplishments of the ancient Persians with great pride. Partly because of this secular (nonreligious) movement and partly because of the survival of the ancient Persian religion, the principal myths associated with that faith became well known by most modern Iranians.

Also, over the course of the centuries, the Persian myths had subtle but important influences on the cultures of peoples living outside of Iran. The society of the earliest Persians was confined mainly to the southern Iranian region bordering the eastern edge of the Persian Gulf. In ancient times that area was known as Fars, or Pars. But eventually, the Persians in a very real sense burst out of their small homeland and became one of the most successful peoples of ancient times. For almost three centuries they had the largest empire the world had yet seen. That mighty and influential realm helped to shape the destinies of dozens of other peoples.

Among those peoples were the veritable founders of Western culture—the Greeks, who conquered the Persian realm in the 330s and 320s B.C. and ruled its remnants for more than two centuries. During that period some Greeks married Persians, and the two cultures mingled. As a result, both the Greeks and through them their own later conquerors, the Romans, absorbed a few Iranian-Persian gods and

This Zoroastrian tower, part of a fire temple, dates from the fifth century B.C. The ancient Zoroastrian religion has survived to this day and is still practiced by a small number of Iranians.

their associated myths. In a similar manner, the ancient Hebrews, who for a while lived under Persian rule, borrowed some key religious concepts from Persian religion. These include life after death and the existence of an evil being who opposes God (known in the West as the devil).

Because some Persian religious concepts had a measurable influence on the development of Western ones, Persian religion and myths remain relevant both inside and outside the Middle East. These religious concepts and the colorful tales associated with them cannot be properly examined, however, without first considering the historical situation of which they were a part. Indeed, a brief overview of the saga of the ancient Persians shows how their religion and mythology developed in the mountainous wilds of Iran. In the words of British scholar John R. Hinnells, "No nation's religion or mythology can be understood in isolation from its historical setting. Some knowledge is needed of the cultural developments and the various influences that were at work. Thus we must turn first to the history of Persia."[1]

CHAPTER 1

Myth and History Intertwined: Persian Origins

The strong connection between the ancient Persians' myths and their everyday lives and beliefs, especially their religious beliefs, can be explained in large part by the fact that they thought those tales were true. Nearly everyone was sure that the gods, demons, and human characters mentioned in the myths were very real. In addition, mythical characters and events were often used by Persian rulers, thinkers, and religious leaders to explain major or dire natural or human events.

When the Sassanian Persian realm fell in the A.D. 600s, for example, the defeated Persians sought in despair to understand how God could allow their country to be virtually erased from the map. The official explanation given by the priests was that the invaders were actually demons, members of the devil's minions. Their victory had been temporary, the story went, and God would someday send a savior to destroy the demons and restore Persia to its rightful place in the human order. Today many people of Persian descent, most of them living in Iran, are still waiting for that heavenly act of salvation to happen. As John R. Hinnells points out, "Myth and history are . . . completely intertwined in [Persian] belief. The Persians understand the whole of their history, past, present, and future, in light of their mythology. History is the stage for the battle between good and evil, and the events which take place on that stage can only be appreciated when seen against the backcloth of God's purpose and nature."[2]

The Stimulus for Creation

This supposed correlation between history and myth can be seen in the way the Persians pictured the creation of their world. At first, earth's surface was flat and flawless, with no mountains or valleys, the story went. The lovely, fertile soil stretched from horizon to horizon, dotted here and there by unspoiled lakes and small seas whose waters were pure, clear, and unmoving. Meanwhile, above in the windless sky loomed the great dome of the heavens, a hard protective shell studded with an array of beautiful, unmoving, shining objects—the sun, moon, and stars. All was tranquil and peaceful and remained that way through the passage of an unknown number of centuries. Then, quite suddenly, as one modern myth teller says, earth's harmonious existence

> was shattered by the entry of evil into the universe. It crashed in through the sky, plunged down into the waters, and then burst up through the center of the Earth, causing the ground to shake and the mountains to grow. . . . It was not only the Earth that was shaken by the entry of evil into the universe. The sun, moon, and constellations were shaken from their place so that they revolve around the Earth . . . entering the sky each day [in] the east [and setting] . . . in the west.[3]

This vivid tale of a peaceful early world unexpectedly disrupted by the appearance of evil is among the most popular of ancient Persia's several creation myths. One reason that it was widely admired and retold over the centuries was that it neatly explained the origin of the peculiar geographic setting in which the Persians lived. Most of Iran, their homeland, is extremely mountainous, with narrow valleys winding their way through the mostly rocky, unforgiving terrain. The central portion of that rugged backdrop consists of the huge Iranian plateau. Elevated from 3,000 to 6,000 feet (914m to 1,829m) above sea level, it stretches more than 600 miles

(966km) from the Caspian Sea in the north to the Persian Gulf in the south. The plateau's several craggy mountain chains, including the Zagros and Hazaran ranges, were (and remain) hard to traverse. Also, their scant or uneven rainfall made farming among them difficult in ancient times.

Stone dwellings perch atop the Iranian plateau beneath the Zagros Mountains. The plateau rises to 6,000 feet above sea level and has numerous mountain ranges.

The Persians were well aware that other kinds of countryside existed. On Iran's eastern flank stretch two large, flat, salt deserts—the Dasht-i Kavir and the Dasht-i Lut. Also, west of the mountainous plateau, on Iran's opposite side, the land drops away into the flat alluvial plains of the valley of the Tigris and Euphrates Rivers, the region called Mesopotamia in ancient times. The distinctly horizontal geography of the deserts and Mesopotamian plains was in stark contrast to the more vertical terrain of the Iranian highlands. The earliest Persians wondered why these landscapes were so different.

The myth of evil's entry into the world provided a convenient answer to that question. Like the parched deserts in the east and fruitful plains in the west, that tale claimed, central Iran had once been flat. Only when the heavens cracked and evil crashed into and burrowed through the ground did the Iranian plateau become a land of jagged extremes in elevation. Furthermore, the fact that the plateau was sandwiched between vast flatter regions suggested to the Persians that the Iranian highlands marked the center of creation. After all, they thought, there had to be a reason that evil landed where it did. Although its appearance had introduced sin into the world, it had also set the rest of creation—including the formation of animals, plants, and humans—in motion. "To the early Persians," scholar Michael Kerrigan writes, "the coming of evil was a stimulus for much in creation. It may have destroyed the blissful changelessness of the [original flat earth], but it did not unleash anarchy. Rather, it released the dynamic rhythms of the world as we understand them today."[4]

Rise of the Medes and Persians

The Persians also felt that myths explained how their nation and its kings and other inhabitants came to be. This belief is reflected in the myths associated with various Persian historical figures, customs, and beliefs. Modern scholars have pieced some of these legendary tales together while compiling a rough sketch of Persian history and culture based on written and archaeological evidence.

Where that history begins—the exact origin of the ancestors of the Persians—is shrouded in the hazy mists of time. But archaeologists have found a few clues that appear to place these ancestors' initial homeland in the region northwest of the Caspian Sea, in west-central Asia. Not long before 1000 B.C., two culturally related tribes, or groups, from that area migrated into Iran. One group, the Mada, now called

Greek-Persian Intermarriage

After conquering Persia, Alexander ordered many of his soldiers to marry Persian women in order to foster understanding between Greeks and Persians. To set an example, he himself married a Persian maiden named Roxane.

This ancient relief depicts the two peoples who settled the Iranian plateau: the Medes (right, in the round hat) and the Persians (left, in cylindrical hat).

the Medes, settled in the northern reaches of the Iranian plateau. The other people, the Parsua, or Persians, moved farther south into Fars.

The Medes made their mark first. In the late 600s and early 500s B.C., they formed a fairly large but short-lived empire that stretched across most of Iran and a few neighboring areas. For a while the Persians were Iranian subjects of the Medes. But in the 550s B.C., a brilliant Persian leader named Cyrus (who reigned as Cyrus II) led his people to a swift victory over the Medes and seized control of the Median capital of Ecbatana, in northwestern Iran.

Cyrus immediately displayed two of the qualities that made him a great king—wisdom and mercy. Instead of destroying or subjugating the Medes, he kept them intact and made their homeland on the plateau a major province of his own new empire. Also, Ecbatana became his second capital (after Pasargadae, in the hills of Fars), and he gave many Median nobles high positions in his royal court. In these ways Cyrus gained the admiration and loyalty of his former enemies and ensured that they would never rise in rebellion.

Cyrus was such a respected and larger-than-life character in the region that as time went by, several myths arose about him. These tales promptly entered the still-growing body of Persian mythology. In one of these popular stories, the king of the Medes, Astyages, had a dream in which he envisioned that a divinely inspired male child would soon be born in his realm. When that boy grew up, he would become like a vine that would spread across all of Asia. When Astyages woke up, his priests interpreted the vine metaphor to mean that the young man would overthrow the Median kingdom and establish a new empire encompassing Iran, Mesopotamia, and the rest of the Middle East.

Fearing he would lose his kingdom, Astyages summoned the man who ran his household, Harpagus. The king ordered Harpagus to seek out the child, kill it, and bury it in a secret place. Herodotus, the fifth-century-B.C.

The Cyrus Cylinder, an account of the conquests of Cyrus I, describes how Cyrus united the Medes and Persians.

Animals for Mothers

In addition to Cyrus, Romulus, and Remus, other characters in ancient myths who were partially raised by animals include the leader of the Greek gods, Zeus, who was raised by a goat, and Paris, a prince of Troy, who was aided by a bear.

Greek historian who included several myths about Cyrus in his famous history book, wrote that Harpagus found the baby and "wept as he took it home." There, he told his wife everything that Astyages had said, and she asked him what he intended to do. "Not," Harpagus replied, "what Astyages has ordered. He can rave and rage as much as he likes . . . but I will not consent to do what he wants. Never will I take a hand in so brutal a murder."[5]

True to his word, Harpagus spared the child, who was given the name Cyrus. Moreover, the mysterious vision from Astyages's dream eventually came to pass. When the boy, whose survival had been ordained by God, grew up, he did indeed overthrow the Median kingdom and establish his own realm, the Persian Empire, in its place.

In another well-known myth about Cyrus, Harpagus found the baby boy in the forest. There, a female dog, guided by God's spirit, had found and fed the child, keeping it alive long enough for a person to find it and raise it in human society. Myths about future kings and heroes being raised by animals in the wild were common in the ancient world. Another familiar example is that of the Italian twin boys Romulus and Remus, the mythical founders of Rome. Like Cyrus, they were condemned to die as infants by a ruler who feared them, and in their case a she-wolf found and raised them until a herdsman happened by and rescued them.

Feats of the Persian Monarchs

Legendary stories about Cyrus aside, he did in fact overthrow Astyages, and by the close of the 500s B.C. the Persian realm was the largest empire in world history up to that time. The first three Persian kings, Cyrus, Cambyses, and Darius I, proved to be strong rulers. They divided up the empire into twenty provinces called satrapies and assigned provincial governors, the satraps, to run them. Although the realm was made up of many conquered lands and peoples, each with its own languages and customs, the central

The Persian Symbol of Authority

Accompanying almost all ancient Persian carvings and inscriptions was an image called the farohar. *It shows a bearded male, perhaps a god, sitting atop a large ring with a bird's wings stretching outward from it. This was apparently a symbol of the authority of either the kingship, Ahura-Mazda, or both. Modern Zoroastrians have adopted the* farohar *as their own symbol, which the late noted scholar of ancient Persia A.T. Olmstead here describes.*

On his head, the bearded god [or man] wears the cylindrical hat, flaring at the top and distinguished from the king's by the horns of divinity and an eight-rayed solar disk. . . . His garment is the draped robe, whose full sleeve curves down to the braceleted wrists. His left hand grasps the ring which bestows sovereignty [authority] on monarchs. His right hand, palm open, is raised in blessing. He is lifted aloft on a huge ring [equipped with] wings. . . . From the ring stretch down objects which have been described as two-forked lightning bolts.

A.T. Olmstead. *History of the Persian Empire.* Chicago: University of Chicago Press, 1970, p. 117.

The farohar *(pictured) was the symbol of the Persian king's divine authority.*

Persian administration managed to hold them all together in a cohesive, moderately efficient whole.

This was partly because the men who ran the central government made several administrative and economic practices standard for all Persians across the empire. For example, all provinces were assigned standard annual tax rates. This ensured that a consistent, dependable amount of wealth entered the imperial treasury each year. Another economic reform that proved highly effective was the adoption of coinage, or the use of coins. (This concept originated in Lydia, in what is now Turkey, one of the regions Cyrus conquered.) Gold Persian coins became known as "darics," after King Darius I.

Darius also introduced an important and impressive engineering feat—a large-scale system of roads. These made it possible for imperial armies and messengers, along with merchants and traders, to travel swiftly from one sector of the realm to another. The best-known Persian road ran for more than 1,500 miles (2,414km). It connected the city of Susa, near the northern end of the Persian Gulf, to Sardis, near the Aegean Sea's coast.

On this new road, which had a surface of hard-packed earth, an average traveler could walk from Susa to Sardis in ninety days. However, the king's couriers, or messengers, covered the distance considerably faster. Darius introduced a system of mounted couriers, who carried political and military communications across the empire on horseback. Riding in relays, like the Pony Express in the early American West, they went from Susa to Sardis in just fifteen days, at the time an almost unbelievable accomplishment. Herodotus, who visited Persia, wrote, "There is nothing in the world which travels faster than these Persian couriers. . . . Nothing keeps these riders from covering their allotted stage in the quickest possible time—neither snow, rain, heat, nor darkness. The first, at the end of his stage, passes the dispatch [message] to the second, the second to the third, and so on along the line."[6]

Other imposing engineering feats created by the Persian monarchs took the form of large-scale artificial canals. For example, Darius built one that ran 125 miles (201km) and connected the Mediterranean Sea to the Red Sea and Indian

Ocean beyond. This waterway expanded trade and prosperity in Egypt and other eastern parts of the Persian realm.

Religious Beliefs and Myths

Such economic and engineering feats were among the leading reasons that the empire was successful. Another was that the Persian monarchs did not force the peoples they conquered to conform completely to Persian customs. In particular, each region was allowed to worship its own gods as it always had. This was widely seen as an enlightened policy and resulted in fewer grievances and rebellions than there might otherwise have been.

As for the religion practiced by the Persians themselves, historians are still somewhat unsure of how the various social classes practiced it. There may have been two or three different versions or levels of the faith, each more orthodox, or formal and strict, than the one below it. According to

A Median officer pays tribute to King Darius. Darius introduced coinage, built roads and canals, and ruled conquered peoples wisely.

some scholars, the Persian priests, called magi, practiced the most orthodox version; the king and nobles followed one a bit less strict; and members of the lower classes had the least orthodox version.

More certain is that in earlier times the Persians had been strictly polytheistic, as they worshipped multiple nature gods they had inherited from their Indo-European ancestors. Scholar Charles Phillips writes, "They worshiped gods and goddesses of fire, water, earth, sky, sun, moon, winds, and storm. They also seem to have hailed divinities of a more abstract nature, who represented qualities such as truth, loyalty, and courage—as well as amoral, warlike deities whose wrath was to be feared."[7]

Among these early deities was a sky god, Ahura-Mazda. Eventually, a great Iranian religious prophet named Zarathustra, whom the Greeks came to call Zoroaster, arose. A monotheist, he preached that Ahura-Mazda, the "Wise Lord," was the one true god. In the most famous myth about this great and infinitely good deity, well before the creation of the present world and humanity, he became embroiled in a long-term struggle with an evil life form or force who was not a god, but a lesser being. That being was named Angra-Mainyu (or Ahriman). From time to time, the two battled each other, for after Ahura-Mazda created the world, Angra-Mainyu continually tried to destroy it. But each time, the one true god intervened and saved the day.

The Myth of Fire's Discovery

By the time Cyrus established the Persian Empire, the Zoroastrian religion built mainly around the worship of Ahura-Mazda had become the official faith of the Persian priests and upper classes. However, they had not abandoned the old gods entirely. Though they no longer formally worshipped them, they still kept and perpetuated the main myths about those early deities as a sort of proud cultural heritage. One current theory is that the version of the faith practiced by the Persian lower classes during the years of the empire involved continued worship of some or all of the old gods, including, of course, Ahura-Mazda.

Whatever differences in religious customs existed in the empire, Persians of all classes revered fire. It was a central symbol of the Persian faith, and people often referred to it as Atar, seeing it, symbolically speaking, as the offspring of Ahura-Mazda. The Persians had ordinary fires, of course, like those in hearths for cooking and warmth and those used to smelt metals and bake pottery. But they also had ritual fires, those used to burn the carcasses of animals when sacrificing to God (Ahura-Mazda) or the old gods. They believed

Zoroaster brings fire and law from the god Ahura-Mazda to the Persians. Fire was sacred in Persian religion.

that the flames carried the smoke, symbolically containing nutrients, up to God (or the gods). So fire, in the guise of Atar, was a sacred path from humans to the divine. An ancient prayer to Atar still used in Zoroastrian worship goes, "I bless the sacrifice and prayer, the good offering, and the wished-for offering, and the devotional offering (offered) unto you, O Fire! son of Ahura-Mazda."[8]

Among the more famous Persian myths was the one that told how both the use and worship of fire got started. In the distant past, the story goes, one of the first human rulers—Hushang, a Persian—was out riding his horse one day when from behind a big boulder came a hideous monster with burning eyes. The beast began to charge, so to defend himself, the man picked up a heavy rock and threw it. Missing the monster, the rock struck the boulder and produced a bright spark, which surprised and scared the creature so much that it ran away. Fascinated rather than afraid, Hushang walked to the boulder and hit it with another rock. Again a spark flew outward. The man had discovered that striking flint produces sparks, which can be used to make fire. That night Hushang and his people celebrated by making a huge bonfire and sending prayers of thanks to Ahura-Mazda. Afterward, the Persians employed fire in their holiest rituals.

The Myths in Later Persian Survivals

All of the Persian kings made sure that this and other cherished myths about the origins of their religious and other customs were perpetuated. Indeed, evidence suggests that the religious stories and practices of the empire in its final years were substantially the same as they had been during the reigns of the first three kings. In contrast, the military and political expertise and accomplishments of the later Persian rulers were far inferior to those of Cyrus, Cambyses, and Darius. Over time poor leadership and other problems plagued the realm, making it easy prey for Alexander the Great, who crossed from Greece into Persian territory in 334 B.C. Within a decade, the last Persian king, Darius III, was dead, and his once enormous and powerful empire was no more.

Herodotus on Persian Sacrifices

The fifth-century-B.C. Greek historian Herodotus wrote fairly extensively about Persian customs, including religious ones. Like the Greeks, he said, the Persians performed sacrifices to their gods. A Persian sacrifice begins, Herodotus wrote, when the worshipper does the following:

Sticks a spray of leaves, usually myrtle leaves, into his headdress, takes his victim to some open place and invokes [calls upon] the deity. . . . The actual worshiper is not permitted to pray for any personal or private blessing, but only for the king and the general good of the community. . . . When he has cut up the animal and cooked it, he makes a little heap of the softest green-stuff he can find, preferably clover, and lays all the meat upon it. This done, a [priest speaks] an incantation over it. . . . Then, after a short interval, the worshiper removes the flesh and does what he pleases with it.

Herodotus. *The Histories*. Translated by Aubrey de Sélincourt. New York: Penguin, 2003, p. 96.

Moreover, the Greeks stayed for a long time. Alexander died suddenly, possibly from alcohol poisoning, in 323 B.C. But in the years that followed, his leading generals fiercely fought one another for control of his new empire, and most of that realm eventually became divided into three large Greek-ruled kingdoms. Nevertheless, in the old Persian heartland in Iran, most people carried on their traditional customs, and the old religious rituals and myths remained largely intact. The same continuation of Persian culture occurred after the Greeks were supplanted by an Iranian people, the Parthians, in the second century B.C.

This had important consequences roughly four centuries later, in the A.D. 240s. At that time a man named Ardashir (who ruled as Ardashir II) defeated the last Parthian king and formed the Sassanian Empire, often called the Neo-Persian

The Literary Golden Age

Many of the old Persian myths were brought together in collections, the most famous being Ferdowsi's *Shahnameh*, in a golden age of literature during the Islamic Abbasid dynasty (family line of rulers), which lasted from A.D. 750 to 1258.

Empire. Because so many Parthian subjects still considered themselves Persians, it did not take long for Ardashir and his followers to reinstate the supremacy of the old Persian ideas, social customs, and religion. Included in the revival of Zoroastrian religion under the Sassanian kings were traditional Persian myths. Many of them were written down in historical annals recounting the long centuries of Persia's past. These writings were products of a golden age of art and literature that flourished under some of the Sassanian monarchs.

Often emphasized, appropriately, in this literary flowering was the Persian myth that explained how writing had originated. In that tale King Tahmures, the son of the early mythical ruler Hushang, who had discovered how to make fire, swore to rid the world of demons. For thirty years Tahmures spent most of his time tracking down and slaying these vile creatures. Finally, he and his followers met the last few thousand of them in a huge battle. Most of the demons were killed in the fighting, and Tahmures had the rest put in chains. The king was planning to destroy the prisoners, but at the last minute he spared them on the condition that they would teach him the art of writing, which the demons knew, but up to then no human did. The demons agreed, and thereafter knowledge of writing spread outward to other human societies and nations.

Dishonesty Is the Worst Flaw

In addition to this and other older Persian myths, some new ones were coined during Sassanian times. The most famous examples were those contained in the collection known as *The Thousand and One Nights*, or more commonly *The Arabian Nights*. Although well known as a famous work of Arab literature, scholars point out that *The Arabian Nights* had a Persian predecessor called *A Thousand Tales*. It consisted of a main story that framed several minor ones. The frame

The mythical queen Scheherazade weaves her tales for the sultan. She would always refrain from telling the end of a tale until the next morning, thereby postponing her beheading.

story is Persian, and the minor tales are mostly Persian, with a few ancient Indian and Mesopotamian myths mixed in.

The frame story is built around an enchanting character, a mythical queen named Scheherazade (or Shehrezad). The events of the tale began when a mythical Persian king named Shahriyar discovered that his wife had been cheating on him. Enraged, he had her executed. Then, still gripped by anger, he decided to take out his wrath on other women as well. As modern myth teller Tony Allan tells it, the vengeful monarch

announced his intention of marrying a new bride every day, only to have her executed at dawn the following morning. For three years Shahriyar lived up to his bloodthirsty pledge, until his realm eventually began to run out of suitable young women. Charged with the job of finding fresh candidates, his vizier [chief administrator] was at his wits' end when Shehrezad, his own daughter, offered herself for the post. [She said that she] had a plan and she insisted on putting it into operation. Her scheme employed her exceptional skills as a story-teller. She counted on whiling away the wedding night with a tale she would leave unfinished at dawn the following morning. The king, she hoped, would be so eager to know the outcome that he would postpone her beheading.[9]

The brave young woman's plan worked. In the morning after she had wed the king, he was excited to know how her story ended, so he allowed her to live another day. This occurred repeatedly as Scheherazade told a new tale each night. She recited a total of one thousand stories, allowing her to survive one thousand days and nights, at which point she ran out of tales to tell. Fortunately for her, by that time King Shahriyar had fallen deeply in love with her. So they lived happily ever after.

At the core of that mythical tale was the Persian king's outrage at having been lied to by his wife. Of course, dishonesty is frowned upon in many cultures. In ancient Persia, however, dishonesty was seen as the worst of all character flaws. One of the surviving statements of King Darius I, who ruled the Persian Empire in the late 500s and early 400s B.C., is, "The follower after falsehood do I detest."[10] This remark reflected a societal attitude toward lying that Herodotus noticed when he visited Babylon, then a major Persian city. The Persians, he wrote, "consider telling lies more disgraceful than anything else, and, next to that, owing money. There are many reasons for their horror of debt, but the chief is their conviction that a man who owes money is bound also to tell lies."[11]

Among the other Persian myths that portrayed lying as evil were those involving the Persian god Ahura-Mazda and his devil-like archenemy, Angra-Mainyu (or Ahriman). In the many mythical stories in which these characters are mentioned, they are repeatedly described in terms of their degrees of honesty. The admirable Ahura-Mazda and his angels are depicted as champions of *Asa*, or "the Truth," whereas the vile Angra-Mainyu is seen as the greatest devotee of *Drug*, meaning "the Lie."

Survival of Persian Culture and Myths

These customs and myths survived the fall of the Sassanian realm to conquering Arab armies in the early 600s. The Persian people, along with their literature and myths, were absorbed into what became a permanent Arab-dominated cultural sphere. Fortunately for the victims of the conquest, the Arabs were highly impressed by Persian culture. As a result, they absorbed numerous aspects of it, thereby

Peinture persépolitaine, représentant le triomphe d'Ormuzd sur Ahriman.

A French copy of a Persian frieze at Persepolis depicts the god Ahura-Mazda in battle with his archenemy, the demon Angra-Mainyu.

keeping it alive. "Within 200 years of the conquest," Phillips points out,

> a new Islamic culture—fusing Arab and Persian influence—was ready to flower. . . . The collision of Arab and Persian culture [produced] an Islamic culture that was the glory of the world at the end of the first millennium A.D. A significant aspect of this cultural renaissance was the emergence of an enriched Persian language that was put to delicate use by later poets and chroniclers.[12]

Some of those later Arab writers penned new collections of the old Persian myths. This made it possible for these tales to survive the rigors of time once more. As a result, they eventually filtered down through a great many generations to modern times, thereby enriching the lives not only of the modern Iranians, but of people around the world.

CHAPTER 2

The Early Gods: Society's Protectors

Zoroaster and the later prophets who described the traditional Persian gods likely had no idea how old those deities actually were. Various evidence found by archaeologists suggests that when the Persians entered Iran somewhat before 1000 B.C., gods like the sky deity Ahura-Mazda and the rain deity Tishtrya had already been worshipped for many centuries. Those divinities had originated among the Indo-European nomads from whom the Persians descended.

To both those nomads and the early Iranian Persians, the gods were not dwellers in a faraway realm, with little or no interest in humans, as the ancient Greeks eventually came to see their own gods. Rather, the traditional Persian deities, though usually invisible, were thought to lurk near or within human society. Many Persians believed that their gods even took a direct, though unseen, role in various rituals of worship. Also, everyone agreed that in various ways these deities protected humans and society from evil.

Some of the myths pertaining to Persia's early gods are gone forever because no written records of them survive. Fortunately, however, enough written sources did survive that modern scholars have been able to piece together a rough picture of those deities, their personalities, and some of their supposed deeds. Of the surviving sources of these myths, the most important was penned by one of the Muslim (or Islamic) writers who, following the Arab conquest of Iran, compiled and retold the Persian myths. Known to us as Ferdowsi (or Firdausi), he was active in the late A.D. 900s. His chief work was a long poem titled the *Shahnameh*, which translates as the *Book of Kings*. For his research, Ferdowsi had access to a number of ancient texts that are now lost, including some Zoroastrian religious writings that retold some of the myths about the gods and their relationships with humans.

Another chief source for these tales is the *Avesta*, the holy book of the Zoroastrian faith. The *Avesta* was first written down in the first few centuries A.D., but most of its contents

A nineteenth-century illustration depicts the birth of the hero Rustam, a story taken from a lost manuscript of the Shahnameh *of Ferdowsi.*

are much older. Among other things, it contains the *Yasht*— a collection of hymns to the early Persian gods, including several myths about these deities. In addition, short versions of a few ancient Persian myths appear in the inscriptions the Persian kings had their scribes carve onto stone tablets, stelae (upright stone or wooden slabs often used as boundary markers), and cliff faces.

The Importance of Sacrifice

The majority of these early Persian deities controlled various aspects of nature, including fire, rain, storms, and the fertility of the soil, all things that directly affected humans and their everyday lives. This was particularly true for the early Asian nomads before they arrived in Iran. Because they moved from place to place and had no towns or elaborate, permanent houses, they were always at the mercy of the natural elements and forces. The myths associated with their gods explained how such forces originated and worked. On the whole, this gave people peace of mind, because something they could explain was less frightening, whereas things that were mysterious and unknown bred suspicion and dread.

The events depicted in the myths about the gods also told people what to expect from these beings. The Persians believed that if they worshipped their gods on a regular basis and, especially, offered them sacrifice, those deities would continue to protect them from demons and other evil forces. The latter were ever eager to harm humans by bringing drought, crop failures, starvation, and other disasters.

But it was not just the *act* of sacrifice that ensured that the gods would keep the evil forces at bay. The Persians believed that the frequency of sacrificial offerings also determined the degree of protection a god would or even could provide. It was thought that each time a sacrifice was performed, it strengthened the god it was aimed at, making it easier for him or her to defeat the powers of evil. Conversely, if fewer sacrifices were performed, the god might grow weaker. In that case the deity might be unable to provide enough protection, and the demons might win out and blight human society in some way. From the Persian religious-mythological

Ancient Persian Religious Writings

The sacred texts of the faith of the ancient Persians remain essential to modern Zoroastrians. The principal religious writing of the faith is the *Avesta*, which was composed over the course of many ancient centuries. The texts of the *Avesta*, consisting primarily of prayers and hymns, contain a number of myths about Ahura-Mazda, Zoroaster, and various gods. Among the component parts of the *Avesta* are the *Gathas*, seventeen hymns of devotion that may have been written by Zoroaster himself. There are also the *Yashts*, hymns directed at both gods and lesser divine spirits; the *Vendidad*, a set of rules for Zoroastrian priests; the *Khordeh Avesta*, a collection of short prayers; and the *Visperad*, a compilation of prayers recited by priests during worship. Other important Persian religious writings that contain myths are the *Denkard*, a collection of stories and religious facts, and the *Bundahishn*, a history of the world from the creation to the Renovation. The *Denkard* and *Bundahishn* were written approximately two centuries after the Arab conquest of Iran in the 600s A.D.

A Zoroastrian priest reads from the Avesta *during a religious ceremony. The text was written over the course of many centuries and contains prayers, hymns, and myths.*

perspective, therefore, regular sacrifice was vital to human civilization. As John R.Hinnells says, "The outcome of the cosmic battle between the forces of life and death depend[ed] on man's faithful observance of his ritual obligations."[13]

The Rain God and the Demon

Thus, to the Persians myths were not simply charming folktales meant to entertain people during leisure hours. They were instead constant reminders that people must remain vigilant and active in matters relating to the gods. If they were not, disaster might well ensue.

A clear example of this relationship between myth and physical worship was contained in the legends of the early Persian god Tishtrya, an important overseer of rain and soil fertility. In these myths, Tishtrya was engaged in a seemingly eternal struggle with the horrible demon of drought, Apaosha.

One of the hymns in the *Yasht* contains the most important myth about Tishtrya, which explains how people could ensure that rain would fall and irrigate their fields. Moreover, the tale outlines the dire consequences if people failed to provide Tishtrya proper worship on a regular basis. In the story, the god took the form of a magnificent white horse with golden ears. Trotting to the shore of a great ocean, he came upon the demon Apaosha, who had also assumed the shape of a horse, this one black. The two beings, their hooves flying to and fro, fought unceasingly for three days and three nights.

At that point, it was clear that Apaosha was winning the battle, so in desperation Tishtrya called out to the creator of all things, Ahura-Mazda, for aid. "Woe is me, O Ahura-Mazda!" Tishtrya cried. "I am in distress [because] men do not worship me with a sacrifice in which I am invoked by my own name! . . . If men had worshipped me with a sacrifice [often enough], I should have taken to me [an enormous amount of] strength!" Hearing this plea, Ahura-Mazda quickly performed a sacrifice to Tishtrya. That crucial act infused the rain god with "the strength of ten horses, the strength of ten camels, the strength of ten bulls, the strength of ten mountains, and the strength of ten rivers."[14]

In fact, Tishtrya became so incredibly strong that he easily defeated the demon. Thereafter, the myth outlined in the hymn concludes, humans saw clearly the importance of sacrificing to the rain god. Raising their hands to him and praying, they recited, "We sacrifice unto Tishtrya, the bright and glorious star, who from the shining east, moves along his long winding course, along the path made by the gods, along the way appointed for him the watery way, at the will of Ahura-Mazda!"[15]

This myth had a great deal of meaning to the average early Persian because it reminded him or her that it was essential not to neglect the performance of the main religious ritual—sacrifice. Indeed, Persians actually viewed this and other rituals, including prayer, as their sacred duty to the gods. It was also a duty to themselves. After all, if people failed to perform the proper sacrifices, one or more gods might, as in the myth, become too weak to fend off evil. In that case evil would make headway, and humanity would be in serious trouble.

Verethragna's Many Physical Guises

According to ancient traditions, the Persian god Verethragna possessed ten incarnations, or physical forms, each of which portrayed a part of his personality or powers. The first was a strong wind. Second was a bull with golden horns and yellow ears. Third was a handsome white horse, and fourth was a powerful camel able to carry extremely heavy loads. Verethragna's fifth incarnation was a male wild boar with large tusks and a mean disposition. The sixth form was a fair-skinned fifteen-year-old boy, and the seventh was a raven that could fly at high speeds. The god's eighth physical guise was a muscular wild ram. The ninth was a male deer skilled in the martial arts, and the tenth was a human male armed with a sword with a golden blade.

The myths also reminded Persian worshippers of the nature of that trouble. In the legendary world described in these stories, if the demons *had* managed to vanquish Tishtrya for good, they would have eliminated rain and thereby ensured that people's crops would not grow. The Persian economy rested primarily on agriculture, so prolonged droughts meant great suffering and certain death for large numbers of people.

Goddess of Waters and Warriors

Although faithfully providing Tishtrya with the proper rituals of worship would likely avert a major drought, it could not ensure that other kinds of disasters would not befall humanity. Fortunately, however, other powerful nature gods were on hand to protect people. One of the more popular was the goddess Ardvi Sura Anahita, often called simply Anahita. On the one hand, she was associated with the waters that flowed through the rivers and oceans. To the ancient Persians, the oceans included what are now known as the Persian Gulf, Indian Ocean, Caspian Sea, and Black Sea.

On the other hand, the Persians believed, Anahita promoted human fertility and reproduction. Supposedly she made male seeds (or sperm) pure enough to produce children and ensured that female wombs would be receptive to those seeds. In a myth recounted in one of the surviving hymns in the *Avesta*, Ahura-Mazda called on the prophet Zoroaster to make sacrifice to Anahita because she was "worthy of sacrifice in the material world, worthy of prayer in the material world; the life-increasing and holy, the herd-increasing and holy, the fold-increasing and holy, the wealth-increasing and holy, the country-increasing and holy; who makes the seed of all males pure, who makes the womb of all females pure for bringing forth [offspring]."[16]

Anahita was also a valiant female warrior. A Persian holy writing listed her soldier-like qualities, saying that she was

Tough Female Warrior Deities

Many modern scholars think that the Persian goddess Anahita was distantly related to the Greek goddess Athena, both having a common ancestor deity. They were both tough female warrior deities, and both the Persians and Greeks were descended from Indo-Europeans from central Asia.

"fair of body, most strong, tall-formed . . . wearing [a] mantle [cloak] fully embroidered with gold. . . . Upon her head [is] a golden crown, with a hundred stars, with eight rays . . . [that can make warriors able to] conquer large kingdoms [and become] clever in turning a chariot round in battle."[17]

Because of Anahita's warlike attributes and ability to instill these same skills in human warriors, Persian soldiers regularly prayed to her and asked her to make them braver, tougher, or more adept in wielding their weapons. It is important to emphasize that during the first several

decades of its existence, the Persian realm founded by Cyrus was known for its effective soldiers and armies. In fact, before the Greeks crushed a Persian army at Marathon (not far from Athens) in 490 B.C., Persian warriors were viewed throughout the Middle East as nearly invincible and widely feared. Many of these renowned Persian soldiers believed that their fighting skills and success in battle derived at least in part from their frequent and earnest prayers and sacrifices to Anahita.

Those warriors knew how one could and should approach the goddess and make requests of her, because some existing myths provided useful tutorials. In one of several such tales described in her primary hymn, a soldier named Tusa prayed to Anahita in the following manner:

> To her did the valiant warrior Tusa offer worship on the back of his horse, begging swiftness for his teams, health for his own body, and that he might watch with full success those who hated him, smite down his foes, and destroy at one stroke his adversaries, his enemies, and those who hated him. He begged of her a boon, saying: "Grant me this, O good, most beneficent Ardvi Sura Anahita! that I may overcome [my enemies in] their fifties and their hundreds, their hundreds and their thousands!" . . . Ardvi Sura Anahita granted him that boon [even] as he was offering her [sacrifice].[18]

Persia's Defeat at Marathon

The famous Battle of Marathon, fought in eastern Greece in 490 B.C., resulted when King Darius I sent an army to punish Athens for earlier interfering in Persian affairs. The Persians lost some 6,400 soldiers in the battle, while the victorious Athenians lost only 192 men.

Divine Champion of Truth

Another warrior deity in the early Persian pantheon, this one male, was Verethragna. He was widely seen as the irresistible force of victory, so Persian soldiers often prayed to him just prior to engaging with the enemy in a battle. Yet this was only one of the god's many guises. In a more specific sense, Verethragna was viewed as the enemy of and fighter against wickedness and untruth. Indeed, he was a genuine champion of truth.

It has been established that telling the truth was seen as a virtue of utmost importance to Persian kings and to many ordinary Persian citizens as well. Granted, honesty was a central pillar of the Zoroastrian faith that arose in the early first millennium B.C, but it is unlikely that this fervent disdain for lying and dishonesty appeared out of nowhere in that period. Indeed, among the Indo-European ancestors of the Persians, the need to be able to trust one's neighbors was paramount. A typical social group in that nomadic culture was small, probably consisting of a few hundred people at best. The group was frequently on the move, and constantly making and breaking camp required great efficiency, which in turn demanded close cooperation. Also, the members of the group had to swiftly assume defensive positions—to circle the wagons, so to speak—when threatened by attackers. In such a close-knit society, an individual who could not be trusted was a serious liability, even a threat, to the community. It is not difficult to see why complete openness and honesty were so valued.

This crucial cultural attribute subsequently passed on through the generations to the Persians in Iran. After Cyrus's armies overran and seized control of the Greek cities of western Anatolia in the 540s B.C., the Persians were shocked at what they viewed as openly dishonest practices by Greeks of all walks of life. According to Herodotus, Cyrus himself described a typical Greek marketplace with scorn, saying it was "a special meeting place in the center of their city where they swear this and that and cheat each other."[19] This so-called deceit among Greek merchants may refer to the fact that they were free to charge whatever they wanted, or whatever they could get, for goods. In contrast, it appears that in Persian markets the king's officers set strict standards of weights and measures. They possibly even set the prices of goods in an attempt to eliminate the chances of merchants cheating their customers.

Verethragna hated cheating and other forms of dishonesty, and the myths associated with him reflect this strong emphasis on honesty and truth telling in Persian society. In a myth cited in the fourteenth hymn of the *Yasht*, Zoroaster asked Ahura-Mazda, "Who is the best-armed of the heavenly gods?" Ahura-Mazda answered, "It is Verethragna." Then, Verethragna himself turned to Zoroaster and said, "I am the strongest in strength; I am the most victorious in victory [and] I shall destroy the malice of all the malicious, the malice of [demons] and men.... [I go] here and there asking . . . 'Who is it who lies [and] thrusts [his oath] against [truth]?' To [that liar] shall I, in my might, impart illness and death!"[20]

Verethragna was such a popular god that, despite the strength of monotheism among the kings and nobles of the Persian Empire, he continued to be worshipped by Persian commoners for many centuries. In fact, people went on sacrificing to him well after the empire's fall to Alexander in the late 300s B.C. Under the Greeks and Parthians who ruled Iran in the centuries that followed, the heroic Verethragna, called Artagnes by the Greeks, was widely identified with two mythical Greek heavenly heroes who were also seen as valiant warriors. They were Ares (the Roman Mars), the Greek god of war; and Heracles (the Roman Hercules), son

A sixth-century-B.C. Achaemenid carving depicts the Greek hero Heracles. The Zoroastrian god Verethragna came to be identified with that muscular hero.

of the chief Greek god, Zeus. Around 69 B.C., a Greek king, Antiochus Theos, who ruled parts of the former Persian realm, erected a statue of Artagnes. Along with that name, the sculptor made sure to chisel those of Ares and Heracles in the inscription on the base.

The Creator of Contracts

Verethragna was long associated with another of the major traditional Persian gods who protected human society—the great sun god Mithra (or Mithras). One reason for this was that Mithra was also unfailingly honest. He is still remembered for this particular trait. In the late twentieth century, while visiting a Zoroastrian community in the Middle East, a Western scholar overheard an elderly woman scolding her granddaughter for fibbing. Mithra was watching, she warned the child, and would know if she lied.

Verethragna and Mithra were also related to each other in a famous myth. In that story Verethragna took the form of a wild boar and ran out ahead of and protected Mithra as the latter rode his fiery chariot, which represented the sun, across the sky each day. Demons frequently attacked Mithra in hopes of extinguishing the sun and shrouding the world in darkness. But as scholar Michael Kerrigan tells it:

> The boar flew into battle before the sun-god, bringing him victory in every fight. With his sharp fangs and steely tusks, he could kill at a single . . . blow, while his hooves and jaw of iron made him an irresistible war machine. . . . Those [evil ones] before him were gored and trampled as he ran forward into a reeking mire of blood and brains mixed with ground-up bones and tufts of matted hair.[21]

As a sun deity who rode a chariot across the sky, Mithra was similar to the early Greek sun god Helios, who also used such a chariot. Indeed, the Greeks came to associate Helios with Mithra. Because of Mithra's role as a deity of truth, the Greeks also associated him with their god Apollo, who was himself described as having the ability to see who was lying or telling the truth.

A Persian relief of the god Mithra, one of the gods that protected human society known for his honesty.

Mithra's role in protecting nature and humanity went well beyond merely bringing light and truth to the world, however. In Persia Mithra was primarily the creator and keeper of contracts, oaths, and covenants. (When used as a noun in ancient Persian, the word *mithra* meant "a contract.") In that capacity, he oversaw a grand contract, or deal, the gods had made with humans, in which humans provided rituals of worship to the gods in return for divine protection against evil.

In Mithra's own case, it was understood that if people gave him the proper sacrifices and prayers, he would continue to make the sun shine. Mithra's task was not easy, as demonstrated in the mythical attacks of demons who wanted to destroy him and extinguish the sun. In one of those stories, one of the most fearsome of all the demons, Azhi Dahaka, assaulted Mithra. But the god, with the aid of his boar friend Verethragna and the fire god Atar, drove the hideous monster away. This myth suggested that Mithra was a heroic individual who constantly risked his own life in order to allow humanity to live in the light. The average Persian therefore believed Mithra was doing humans a huge favor and that it was only right to repay that selfless act by providing the god with regular sacrifice.

Rewarding the Faithful

Mithra was also known to reward the faithful and punish the unfaithful. This likely made some Persians think twice about doubting the existence of Mithra and the other gods. Various brief myths in the *Avesta* support this cautious approach to religious belief. In one of these tales, which appears in a hymn dedicated to Mithra in the *Yasht*, Zoroaster and Ahura-Mazda conferred about Mithra. In answer to the prophet's queries, Ahura-Mazda said that Mithra was "as worthy of prayer as myself." Moreover, humans must not fail to do their duty to the gods, as agreed to in the deal made long ago by Mithra. "Break not the contract," Ahura-Mazda declared. "To Mithra all the faithful worshipers of [Ahura] Mazda must give strength and energy with [their sacrifices]. Let the faithful man drink of the [sacrificial wine] cleanly prepared, which if he does, [and] if he offers [it] unto Mithra, [that god] will be pleased with him and without anger."[22]

Like Verethragna, Mithra was so popular that he survived the Persian Empire's fall and continued to be worshipped both in Iran and other parts of the Middle East. Mithra's later worship far surpassed that of Verethragna, however. The Romans adopted Mithra's cult in the first century A.D. (or perhaps somewhat earlier), and worship of the god spread throughout Rome's European and North African provinces. The nature of Roman worship of Mithra, which seems to have differed in some ways from the Persian version, remains unclear and is hotly debated by modern scholars. What is certain is that the god's main myth in Roman eyes involved

Roman Worship of Mithras

The ancient Romans worshipped the Persian god Mithra as Mithras. How this came to be remains uncertain. One theory is that after Rome conquered Anatolia and other regions that had earlier been parts of the Persian Empire, men living in those regions were recruited into the Roman army. They carried their worship of Mithra with them, and over time they converted some of their fellow soldiers in various corners of the Roman Empire. This scenario is likely because the deity's cult was always stron-gest among the army ranks. Roman worship of Mithras reached its peak roughly from A.D. 100 to 400. In art, for reasons unknown, the god was shown being born as a young man rather than as an infant. Usually Mithras carried a torch or a knife. He used that knife to kill a large bull, his chief feat in the numerous carvings and paintings depicting him. The exact reasons for Mithras's slaying of the bull remain unclear, mainly because any Roman writings that may have explained that particular myth have not survived.

A Roman sculpture of the god Mithras slaying a bull. The Persian cult of Mithras became popular with Roman soldiers.

his hunting, riding, wrestling, and finally killing a large bull. Afterward, he slaughtered the beast and consumed its flesh in a feast shared by the Roman sun god Sol. The meaning of this myth remains unclear. But it does illustrate how an extremely ancient god who originated in central Asia could make his way to Persia and later across the known world, in large part through the enduring, powerful allure of his myths.

CHAPTER 3

Persia's Mythical Kings and Heroes

S everal of the better-known stories in Persian mythology deal with the exploits of Iran's legendary early kings. The inhabitants of the Persian Empire founded by Cyrus in the 500s B.C. believed that their present rulers were in a sense modern-day continuations of a line of kings from the dimly remembered past. It was thought that those early monarchs had established the basic social institutions and customs of human civilization. In fact, the first of those early kings had supposedly been fashioned by Ahura-Mazda when that god had created the world.

The myths about the early kings were not simply pleasant tales to tell in front of the family hearth after dinner. Rather, these stories had a great deal of relevance to the lives of the Persian people because they helped to determine how the real Persian kings would rule their subjects. First, these stories explained the key duties a king owed his people. According to both religion and mythology, the king's authority to rule came directly from God, or Ahura-Mazda. This authority, called the *farr*, or "Divine Glory," also interpreted as a heavenly glow shining around the ruler's head, could be stripped away from a bad king. This actually happened in a myth in which Ahura-Mazda judged a king unworthy of the *farr* and bestowed it instead on an accomplished hero.

The latter was only one of several larger-than-life human champions inhabiting the Persian myths.

Another way the myths about the early kings were relevant to Persian society was that these rulers were seen as prototypes, or models, for the real Persian kings. The legendary rulers set an example, and Persian citizens often expected the reigning king to live up to that example. So it was not unusual for a king to consciously imitate one of the mythical monarchs and to compare himself favorably with that ruler.

A Persian king receives the crown from Ahura-Mazda. The ancient Persians believed the king's authority came from the deity himself.

The Ideal King

Of these early kingly prototypes, none was more revered and imitated than Yima, who was said to be the first human king in some Persian myths. (A few alternate myths featured different individuals in the role of the first human ruler.) Yima's sterling reputation was built around a myth in which he ruled for one thousand years. During that period there was widespread peace; everyone had plenty of food, so hunger was unheard-of, and demons and other evil forces were kept away from human society.

The world was so prosperous under Yima's enlightened rule that parents could afford to raise as many children as they wanted, so most couples had numerous offspring. That caused the population to increase so much that the earth became terribly overcrowded. Yima was not in the least worried, however. He knew that Ahura-Mazda, in his great wisdom and love for humanity, would endow the king with whatever powers he needed to rectify the situation. According to one modern mythologist:

> Yima merely took his ring and dagger and pressed them into the ground. Then he commanded the Earth to open and outstretch itself. . . . The ground beneath him creaked and shuddered in response and was [torn] from side to side [and] the horizons seemed to retreat on every front as the world extended itself by a third. Now it seemed there would be ample space for any number of human and animal inhabitants.[23]

Myths of Original Sin

Considering Yima's impressive achievements, it is no wonder that he was seen as a hero as well as a monarch and that the real Persian kings sought to live up to the ideals he had set. There was one incident in Yima's story, however, that they did not desire to replicate. This was an outburst of extreme self-importance and overconfidence that occurred toward the end of his tenure as king. Apparently, as told in another myth about Yima, his uncounted good deeds and successes finally went to his head, and he began claiming to be as good and powerful as God himself. According to one ancient source:

> Yima summoned all the high officials and told them: "The world is mine [because] the royal throne has never seen a king like me, for I have decked the world with excellence and fashioned Earth according to my will. . . . Who dares to say that there is any greater king than me? [Humanity owes] me sense, and life, and everything. Those who do not love me are followers of the . . . Evil One. So now you must hail me as the maker of the world and worship me!"[24]

Yima soon realized that he had made a colossal mistake, for in Ahura-Mazda's eyes it was a sin for a human to equate himself with God. As a punishment, Ahura-Mazda removed from Yima the *farr*, the awe-inspiring radiance that surrounded that ruler's body, and provided him with his kingly authority. Under these circumstances, Yima could no longer serve as king, and his people were sorely disappointed in him.

In contrast, the horrifying demon Azhi Dahaka chortled with glee when he heard what had happened. For a long time Yima had been strong enough to keep the evil beings and forces, including Azhi, at bay. But now, thanks to his sin and punishment, Yima had been fatally weakened. Seeing his chance, Azhi drove Yima from his palace and seized the throne. Fortunately for humanity, however, a young hero named Thraetaona (also known as Faridun) arrived on the scene and vanquished the slithering demon. Ahura-Mazda then bestowed the *farr* on Thraetaona, who thereby became king and brought righteousness and happiness back to the world.

In ancient Persian society and religion, Yima's awful mistake—to liken himself to God—was viewed as an example of original sin. That is, it was the first major sin committed by a human and as such the prototype for all later human sins. The Persians had an alternate myth that featured a first couple, who disobeyed and disrespected Ahura-Mazda,

Groveling Before the King

The act of prostration before the Persian king, as well as by ordinary Persians before members of the upper classes, shocked most Greeks when they witnessed it. The Greeks saw the act, called proskenysis, *as degrading for a free individual. In this passage from his* Anabasis, *the Greek historian Arrian recalls the words of Callisthenes, one of the officers of Alexander the Great, on the subject.*

There is a difference between honoring a man and worshipping a god. The distinction between the two has been marked in many ways, for instance, by the building of temples, the erection of statues, the dedication of sacred ground. All these are for the gods. . . . Yet of all these things not one is so important as this very custom of prostration. . . . A god, far above us on his mysterious throne, it is not lawful for us to touch. And that is why we proffer him the homage of bowing to the earth before him. . . . It is wrong, therefore, to ignore these distinctions. We ought not to make a man look bigger than he is by paying him excessive and extravagant honor, or, at the same time, impiously to degrade the gods . . . by putting them in this matter on the same level as men.

Arrian. *Anabasis Alexandri*. Published as *The Campaigns of Alexander*. Translated by Aubrey de Sélincourt. New York: Penguin, 1976, pp. 219–220.

Subjects prostrate themselves before the Persian king, an act the ancient Greeks found degrading.

much like the biblical Adam and Eve disobeyed God. That misdeed from the distant past was also sometimes called the original sin. These myths played a role in Persian society similar to the one played by the tale of Adam and Eve in the Bible. Namely, they explained to the average devoutly religious Persian how humanity, which was supposedly once innocent, pure, and unspoiled, became corrupted. Thereafter, it was thought, each person in each new generation had the potential to commit wrongdoing. But God expected him or her to always be on guard and resist the temptation to sin, or else suffer divine punishment as Yima had.

Good Versus Evil

Part of the penalty Yima had paid for his offense against God was to be assaulted by the wicked demon Azhi Dahaka. In fact, nearly all of the Persian myths dealing with the early kings and heroes contain confrontations between good and evil forces. In the most popular Persian creation myth, for example, the first human king must confront the most powerful of all evil forces in the Persian belief system—Angra-Mainyu. In this story the first king, Gayo-maretan (or Kayumars), is also the first human being.

In the ages before Gayo-maretan's creation, Ahura-Mazda dwelled in a heavenly kingdom filled with incredibly bright light. Meanwhile, far below in a dismal, dark place, lived Angra-Mainyu. The evil one was powerful, but he was also ignorant and had no inkling of the existence of light and goodness far above him. In contrast, Ahura-Mazda, in his great wisdom, was well aware of Angra-Mainyu's existence and decided to create a world in which he could confront and defeat that dark being.

Ahura-Mazda began by flooding the universe with dazzling light. Disturbed by this radiance, Angra-Mainyu tried to extinguish it but could not. At that moment Ahura-Mazda revealed himself to the evil one and offered a deal in which Angra-Mainyu would learn to live

The First Sin

The sin committed by the world's first couple, Mashye (mash-YUH) and Mashyane (mash-YUH-nuh), in Persian mythology was to name the evil Angra-Mainyu, rather than Ahura-Mazda, as their creator.

A Persian hero/ king slays a demon dragon. Most Persian myths about early kings and heroes contain a confrontation between good and evil.

in light and goodness, and in exchange Ahura-Mazda would not destroy him. The vain, conceited, and short-sighted Angra-Mainyu refused to accept this bargain, however, and returned to his dark abode. There he molded an army of demons to help him oppose Ahura-Mazda.

Ahura-Mazda proceeded to create the world, and in its center he placed Gayo-maretan. This first person ruled the flat earth, still devoid of people other than himself, for three thousand years, at which point Angra-Mainyu crashed through the sky and caused the mountains and valleys to form. The evil one also unleashed all manner of repulsive creatures, among them snakes, scorpions, and lizards. In addition, Angra-Mainyu heaped ills and vices—including disease, hate, pain, hunger, and greed—on poor Gayo-maretan. The king managed to ward off the frightening fiend for thirty years but eventually succumbed to his attacks and collapsed, dead, in the dirt. All was not lost, however, for Ahura-Mazda descended and infused the man's remains with golden light, purifying and warming them. In scholar Charles Phillips's words,

> For forty years the sun shone brightly on that same spot and eventually a rhubarb plant forced its way from the soil. The plant's stalks and leaves then became the bodies and limbs of a man and woman, Mashya and Mashyanag, who were father and mother . . . of humankind. The human couple soon broke free of the plant's roots to walk upon the Earth.[25]

This creation story was important to Persia's kings because it established that the first king had been directly created and loved by God. That made the kingship a holy institution rather than a mere mortal creation. Also, although Gayo-maretan had been killed by Angra-Mainyu, that first king's body had, with God's help, made it possible for the human race to spring forth from the ground. In a way, this made Gayo-maretan the father of humanity. A Persian king, and later a Sassanian one, could claim that, just as the legendary first king had been the father of all later humans, the present ruler of Persia was the father of all his subjects. Moreover, this relationship of father to children had been blessed by Ahura-Mazda himself. So no Persian subject should be so bold and unwise as to doubt the king's right to rule over him and to demand from him absolute obedience.

Based on these ideas, in practice the Persian king was seen "as God's special representative, working under his protection," as one historian puts it. The king

Yima's Sad Fate

In the myth of the Persian king Yima's great sin against God, the demon Azhi Dahaka drove Yima from his throne. There is another part of that myth, sometimes told as a separate tale, in which the demon goes further and hunts down the former human king. As long as Yima remained alive, Azhi reasoned, the chance existed that he might find a way to retake his throne. So for many decades the demon marshaled his evil assistants in a search for the aging man. Finally, when Yima was quite elderly, someone recognized him, and Azhi's forces captured him. Wasting no time, the demon had his henchmen saw poor Yima in half, starting at the top of his head and going straight downward. With Yima dead, Azhi Dahaka felt that nothing could dislodge him from the throne and that he would surely rule humanity with an iron fist for all eternity. As it turned out, that horrifying situation never came to pass, as the heroic Thraetaona arrived, defeated him, and imprisoned him inside a mountain.

was so exalted that his face was masked before the people, his presence concealed behind a curtain and ordinary men prostrated themselves [laid facedown on the ground or floor] before him. [The Persians] appear to have transferred myth into history and in their mythical symbols expressed their conviction that the good king manifests the [spirit] of God.[26]

As for ordinary Persians, the creation myth featuring Gayo-maretan served a special purpose. The ancient Persians relied on their creation myths to explain how the world they knew, along with themselves, had come to be. Parents told their children and teachers told their students these stories in each new generation, thereby keeping the myths alive and relevant in century after century. That process never stopped, and today children in families that practice

The Persian king Darius receives homage in this relief. The creation myth taught that the king was created by God and thus was God's special representative.

the Zoroastrian faith still learn about the mythical Iranian kings and their roles in making the human race possible.

Saving the World

Among the most important of these myths is one in which Yima saves the world, thereby preserving humanity when it is threatened with extinction. Its events, which appear in the *Vendidad*, part of the *Avesta*, take place before his great sin and fall from grace. As the story begins, Yima had already ruled for nine hundred years, during which he had enlarged the earth to accommodate more people and animals and made all the humans then living content. The climate was always warm and pleasant, and food grew in abundance.

But this agreeable situation was not destined to last forever. With the passage of each year, the evil being Angra-Mainyu grew increasingly jealous and angry over Yima's success and humankind's happiness. Determined to ruin things and cause as much misery as possible, Angra-Mainyu planned to plunge the world into three successive, devastatingly cold winters. These plans were made in secret. But as usual, the all-knowing Ahura-Mazda was instantly aware of them. He hurried to Yima, warned him of what was coming, and advised him to construct a *vara*, a cave-like shelter that would protect some selected people and animals. Ahura-Mazda said:

> O fair Yima . . . upon the material world [three] evil winters are about to fall, that shall bring the fierce, deadly frost [and] make snow-flakes fall thick [and] deep on the highest tops of mountains. . . . Therefore make you a *vara* [2 miles, or 3.2km] long . . . on every side of the square [for a total of 4 square miles, or 10.36 sq km]. And [into it] bring the seeds of sheep and oxen, of men, of dogs, of birds, and of [other species]. There you shall establish dwelling-places, consisting of a house with a balcony, a courtyard, and a gallery [and] bring the seeds of men and women, of the greatest, best, and finest on this earth. [You] shall bring the seeds of every kind of tree [and] every kind of fruit. . . . All those [things] shall you bring [into] the *vara*.[27]

Yima did as God instructed. The king made sure that inside the *vara* there were houses for the people, pens for the animals, and a stream to supply water to both humans and beasts. Having built a small city and well-stocked countryside inside the protected enclosure, Yima's first task was finished. His second duty was to look after the residents of the *vara* during the terrible winters. The latter were so cold that all living things outside the *vara* froze to death. Finally, the awful arctic blasts ended and warmth returned to the world. Out of the *vara* stepped Yima, followed by the people and animals he had saved, and they proceeded to replenish the barren lands.

Oral Tales Preserved?

Numerous scholars, from the Middle Ages up to the present, have pointed out the close similarity between this story and other tales from the Middle East about humanity surviving a huge catastrophe. In particular, Yima's tale resembles the tales of the great flood, in which God warns a man (Ziusudra in the Sumerian version, Utnapishtim in the Babylonian version, and Noah in the Hebrew version) of the coming deluge. In those stories, the man constructs an ark, or large boat, in which he places a few people and two of every animal.

It is difficult to know for sure which version of the story came first. Most experts think the Sumerian one was the original and that the others, including the Persian one, were later adaptations. However, the version featuring Yima stands out for its use of extreme cold as the destroying force as opposed to raging flood waters.

One possibility some scholars have suggested is that the Persian version did indeed materialize centuries after the other versions. However, that myth's core images—of a small group of people surviving a series of harsh winters by erecting a shelter—may be extremely ancient. These aspects of the story may be distant folk memories passed down through hundreds of generations by word of mouth from the early Indo-Europeans who gave rise to the Persians. That nomadic group hailed from central Asia, which experiences very cold, harsh winters. It may be that a long series of colder-than-normal winters there motivated the Persians' ancestors to migrate southward into Iran. Meanwhile, the memories of that great freeze were preserved in a myth that later merged with the Mesopotamian flood legend. If this scenario did occur, it demonstrates how a changing climate and its large-scale physical effects can be preserved in oral tales that over the passage of time morph into myths. In this case the details of the myth reflected the real-life experiences not of the Persians themselves, but of their distant ancestors.

Some Well-Chosen Myths

In whatever manner that myth originated, it proved highly instructive to a young Persian learning about his or her culture and its religious beliefs. Unlike the Hebrew version of the story, in which God grows angry and sends the flood to punish humanity, the Persian version envisions a more

beneficent deity. The coming catastrophe is not the work of Ahura-Mazda, but rather of the evil one, Angra-Mainyu.

The frequent emphasis that ancient Persian religion and mythology place on evil and the dangers it poses to humans was crucial to the way people saw both God and themselves. The average Persian was brought up to be a good person who always told the truth. But parents, priests, and other elders also drummed into children the idea that evil was not only real but always lurking nearby, eager to corrupt and destroy whoever it could.

To illustrate this supposed negative fact of life to a new generation, the older generation used some well-chosen myths. These stories portrayed evil beings, especially demons, attacking, kidnapping, imprisoning, killing, and/or

Ziusudra tells Gilgamesh how his ark came to rest on a mountain after the Great Flood. The Persian myth of Yima and his vara is thought to be based partly on the Sumerian legend of Gilgamesh.

eating people. The same stories invariably contained human heroes like Thraetaona. They represented the force of goodness, in a sense an earthly manifestation, or guise, of Ahura-Mazda's own pure and righteous powers.

In addition, the myths of good and evil often contained images that reflected the physical realities of highly mountainous Iran. The evil creatures frequently lived atop or inside mountains, or they held their victims prisoner in caves in the mountains, or the heroes eliminated the monsters by imprisoning them inside rocky mountainsides. After defeating Azhi Dahaka, for instance, Thraetaona tunneled deep inside a hillside, tossed the demon into a dark cave, and then used solid rock to fill in the only escape shaft.

Stalwart Rustam

Azhi Dahaka was only one of many demons who threatened human society, however. So danger still lurked in various dark corners of the world. One of these horrid creatures, Div-e-Sepid by name, but better known as the White Demon, sometimes preyed on traders and other travelers who journeyed back and forth between Iran and the Caspian Sea.

This illustration depicts Rustam slaying the White Demon in a cave.

In the chief myth about that revolting creature, one day the reigning Persian king, Kay Kavus, decided to lead a small army of soldiers in the conquest of the little-known land of Mazinderan, near the Caspian Sea. Hearing about the expedition, the renowned hero Zal went to the palace and urged the king to abandon the venture. It would be too dangerous, Zal said, because the forests along the road leading northward were infested with demons. But the overconfident Kay Kavus ignored Zal and launched the expedition.

It turned out that Zal had been right to caution the king. As the Persian army approached the Caspian Sea, the forests suddenly grew dark and quiet. Soon "a huge storm gathered," modern myth teller Norma L. Goodrich writes.

Then the storm burst. In an explosive onslaught it blew across the flat tableland where the Persians huddled unprotected. . . . [Things became so chaotic that] Kay Kavus and his soldiers . . . could not even see the face of the White Demon when it appeared leering and ghostly white at the horizon's edge. They surrendered quietly to his 12,000 demons, who ripped off their jeweled collars and rings and tore their weapons from their sides.[28]

When Zal heard that the king and his troops had been captured, he wanted to rush to the rescue. But he had grown too old and frail to be of any help, so he notified his son Rustam (or Rostam), who had recently proved to be an even greater hero than Zal. Rustam sped across the mountains and deserts and found that the White Demon was holding the king in a cave inside a mountain. The fearless young man tore the head off the demon guarding the cave and tossed the gory object into the midst of the other demons. They panicked and scurried away, screaming as they went. After rescuing the king, Rustam tracked down and slew the White Demon, a courageous deed that earned him the praise of all Persians. His admirers lived not only in the mythical world that he, Zal, and Kay Kavus inhabited, but also in real Persian society. There, all young boys wanted to grow up to be as brave, honest, and god-fearing as stalwart Rustam. Such was the power of myths in the ancient world.

Rustam's Trusty Horse

The great mythical Persian hero Rustam was often supported and aided by his trusty and equally heroic horse, Rakhsh, whose name means "luminous" in Persian. It was said that no one could tame the steed but Rustam, indicating they were made for each other.

CHAPTER 4

The Myths and Realities of Zoroaster

Among the most popular and important of the ancient Persian myths are those that deal with the life and deeds of the prophet Zoroaster (also called Zarathustra or Zardosht), founder of the primary faith practiced in the Persian and Sassanian Empires. He was not the only major historical figure about whom the Persians developed myths. Among several others were Cyrus, founder of the Persian Empire, and Alexander the Great, that realm's ultimate conqueror. Zoroaster lived long before these men, probably sometime between 1400 and 1000 B.C. For that reason and also because he delved into the mysteries of religion, he generated a considerably larger number of legends than they did.

Indeed, many dozens of myths, most of them short but some longer, have survived about Zoroaster and the faith he founded. Some describe his birth and life; others recount the miracles he was said to have performed; and still others depict him interacting with Ahura-Mazda, various traditional Persian gods, and God's heavenly angels, the Amesha Spenta. Finally, a few of these myths tell how the prophet will be indirectly involved in the epic events the Zoroastrians believe will occur in the future when God at last confronts and destroys evil.

The Prophet's Teachings

Zoroaster's basic teachings, as outlined in these myths, revolve around the contrast between good and evil. He was essentially a monotheist who held that Ahura-Mazda was the one true god and that God had long been engaged in a struggle with evil, personified by the dastardly Angra-Mainyu. Humans needed to choose between those extremes, he said, and by choosing the good—represented by Ahura-Mazda— one would be assured of spending eternity in heaven. Also, with the exception of Ahura-Mazda, the older gods who had

A depiction of the prophet Zoroaster, whose teachings, as told in the myths, revolve around the battle between good and evil.

been worshipped before Zoroaster's time were actually *daevas*, or false deities inspired by Angra-Mainyu to confuse people. The devout must constantly be on guard, Zoroaster said, to avoid being misled by the *daevas*. So human life was a struggle similar to that in which God himself was engaged—a battle between the forces that wanted to help and enlighten people and those that desired to corrupt them.

The older Indo-European gods—Tishtrya, Anahita, and the others—were not completely demoted or abandoned in the centuries that followed Zoroaster's lifetime, however. Later religious leaders understood that the Persians' belief in the older gods was deeply ingrained in society and realized that it was not realistic to simply declare those deities false while promoting belief in a single god.

As a result, over time the myths of the older gods became interwoven into Zoroaster's own teachings and myths, as well as into the tales about Ahura-Mazda and the ongoing fight between good and evil. The older gods and their stories became instructive in understanding everyday religious rituals and morality. In this way it became acceptable to talk about the traditional gods and their myths while embracing the idea that Ahura-Mazda was the sole god.

A Miraculous Birth

It is unknown whether Zoroaster realized that over time he too would become the subject of various myths. But that is what indeed came to pass. After his death, as the centuries wore on, the events of his life became material for many important Zoroastrian myths. (Today some Zoroastrians think those myths describe real events. Others feel that they are a mixture of true and legendary happenings.)

The myth of his conception and birth is a good example. In it Ahura-Mazda decided to reveal that he was the one true god through the voice of a human prophet. So the deity sent the Divine Glory—the mystical glow that makes the stars shine—down to the hearth of the home of a human couple. From the hearth, the light leaped into the body of the woman. Later, when she gave birth to a daughter named Dughdhova, the little girl's own body pulsated with that heavenly light, which made her glow in the dark.

In the myth of Zoroaster's conception and birth, depicted here, Ahura-Mazda decides to reveal that he is the one true God through the voice of his prophet.

Soon Angra-Mainyu learned about the little girl and, hoping to thwart God's plan, the evil one inflicted her village with disease and natural disasters. At the same time, demons whispered in the ears of the local elders, telling them these ills had been caused by Dughdhova. To keep the girl safe, therefore, her father sent her to live in another, faraway village.

In her new home Dughdhova grew up and married a man named Pourushaspa. Not long after the wedding, she realized that she was with child, and nine months later a

Good and Evil Creatures

The magi zealously preached that some animals, such as dogs and cattle, were good, whereas certain others were vile followers of Angra-Mainyu and therefore must be destroyed whenever possible. High on the list of these supposedly evil creatures were creeping critters such as earthworms, ants, flies, frogs, and snakes.

boy was born. According to the *Denkard*, a ninth- or tenth-century text about Persian religion that contains a biography of Zoroaster, "One marvel is this which is declared, that on being born [the child] laughed outright. The seven midwives who sat around him were quite frightened . . . [by the laugh and by the] radiance [that] was openly seen [around him]."[29] It turned out that the infant Zoroaster laughed because he was already aware of his great religious mission to humanity.

By the time that King Cyrus established the Persian Empire and adopted Zoroastrianism as its official faith, this myth of the prophet's miraculous birth had passed through numerous generations. It had come to inspire the faithful in the same way that the story of Jesus's birth in a stable inspires Christian believers today. The idea that Zoroaster had come into the world under special, divinely inspired circumstances was a powerful incentive to believe in the precepts of the Persian Empire's primary religion.

Zoroaster's Mission

A series of myths, including those about Zoroaster's survival against attempts on his life, his performance of miracles, and his meetings with angels and God, served a similar purpose for the faithful. Each confirmed that the prophet was no ordinary person. Rather, he was God's chosen one, who received that deity's protection and was even allowed to meet the creator of the universe face-to-face.

For example, several myths told about how Angra-Mainyu, having failed to destroy Zoroaster's mother, endeavored to kill the young prophet while he was growing up. In one story the evil one sent demons to poison Pourushaspa's mind and make him think his son was an evil spirit. In a trance, the father placed the child on a pile of wood and set it on fire. Zoroaster was protected by God, however, so the flames refused to touch the boy's skin. In another tale, the father threw Zoroaster into the cave in which a vicious she-wolf made her den. But once more, the child received divine protection, for the mother wolf took a liking to the boy and cared for him as if he was one of her own offspring.

As told in another myth about Zoroaster's life, when he had grown into an ethical young man, he received a visit from Ahura-Mazda's angel Vohu Manah. One of the six Amesha Spentas, Vohu Manah, often called Good Mind, was said to sit on God's right hand and offer him advice when asked. This important spirit of goodness also had the task of keeping a daily record of the thoughts, words, and actions of each human.

Finally, it was Vohu Manah's job to lead human souls to God, which explains why he appeared to Zoroaster. According to a passage in the *Denkard*, Zoroaster asked Vohu Manah who he was and why he had come. The angel replied that the man was going to "confer with him by whom you [were] produced and by whom I [was] produced, who is

Ahura-Mazda and Angra-Mainyu dispute who has dominion over the world. Zoroaster's teachings were based on the struggle between good and evil.

the most propitious [benevolent] of spirits, who is the most beneficent of existences."[30] The "him" to whom Vohu Manah referred was, of course, Ahura-Mazda. Zoroaster then met with God, who explained that it was the man's destiny to become a prophet and begin to enlighten humanity about Ahura-Mazda's teachings.

Zoroaster eagerly accepted this mission and began teaching. Most people ignored or condemned him at first, as they felt his ideas ran contrary to their existing beliefs. But eventually he made an important conversion. King Vishtaspa, ruler of a kingdom in central Asia, had a favorite horse that had become badly crippled and was suffering. Zoroaster made a deal with the king, which stipulated that if the prophet could heal the horse, Vishtaspa would gladly convert. Aided by Ahura-Mazda's powers, Zoroaster performed a miracle by restoring the horse to perfect health. So the king, true to his word, became an ardent follower of Ahura-Mazda as the one true god. The prophet was said to have performed other similar miraculous feats during his long life.

Myths of Heaven and Hell

While the myths about Zoroaster's personal life inspired many Persians to adopt and follow the worship of Ahura-Mazda, other myths associated with Zoroastrianism gave them hope for the future. Part of that future had to do with the personal fate of each human after death. The other aspect of the future predicted in the Zoroastrian myths deals with the fate of the entire world and humanity as a whole.

Regarding the fates of individuals, Zoroaster claimed that after a person dies, the soul floats above the body for three days and three nights. During that interval, evil spirits loom close and attempt to inflict terrible pain on the soul. However, the prayers and sacrifices of the deceased's relatives and friends have the power to protect the soul from this particular threat.

In the next part of the myth of the afterlife, the soul is judged by three of the Yazatas, minor angels who were ranked as gods in the pre-Zoroastrian Iranian pantheon. These divine judges are Sraosha, Rashnu, and Mithra. They weigh the good thoughts and deeds and bad thoughts and deeds that have occurred during the person's life, and if the good thoughts and deeds are more numerous than the bad ones, the soul goes to heaven. In contrast, if the bad outweigh the good, the soul goes to hell.

Another set of related myths appear in the Zoroastrian writing known as *The Book of Arda Viraf*, which evidence suggests dates from Iran's Sassanian era. It tells how the title character, a good, god-fearing follower of Zoroaster and believer in Ahura-Mazda, received a heavenly vision. The purpose of the vision was to allow him to visit heaven and hell and see what was happening in both. He was then expected to pass his experiences on to other worshippers so they could know what to expect in the afterlife and shape their lives accordingly. In this tale, after returning from heaven, Viraf said that he

Persian Burial Methods

To dispose of their dead, most ancient Persians dipped the body in wax and buried it. A few in the upper classes, including King Darius I, opted to be interred in stone tombs. In both cases the Zoroastrian religious rule saying that the corpse should not touch and thereby contaminate the earth was upheld.

saw the souls of the [pious], who walked adorned [in beautiful clothes] and were above the other souls in all splendor. And Ahura-Mazda ever exalts the souls of the [pious], who are brilliant and elevated and mighty. And I said "Happy are you who are a soul of the [pious], and it seemed to me sublime." I also saw the souls of those who, in the world . . . were steadfast in the good religion of Ahura-Mazda, which [that god] taught to Zoroaster. When I advanced, they were in gold-embroidered and silver-embroidered clothes, the most embellished of all clothing. And it seemed to me very sublime. . . . I also saw the souls of good rulers and monarchs, who ever increased their greatness, goodness, power, and triumph thereby, when they walked in splendor, in their golden trousers. [And] I also saw the souls of the great and of truthful speakers, who walked in lofty splendor with great glory. And it seemed to me sublime.[31]

Myths: True, False, or Symbolic?

It is important to consider the meaning of the word *myth* as the ancient Persians understood it and as modern Zoroastrians understand it. Most people today rather casually employ the word to mean a story that is not true, as opposed to one that is known to be factual. Thus, it is common for Jews, Christians, and Muslims—all monotheists—to group ancient Greek, Roman, Egyptian, and Persian myths together as fanciful stories concocted in bygone ages by people who were ignorant of the existence of a single, all-powerful god. Moreover, a Jew, Christian, or Muslim would be offended if someone referred to a tale from the Old Testament, New Testament, or Quran as a myth. In contrast, Zoroastrians, like the Hindus and members of some other faiths, see myths simply as colorful tales that explain or illuminate the origins, prophecies, and inner workings of their faith. Some think those stories *are* true, or nearly so, or else that they symbolize certain universal religious truths. They are therefore not insulted when someone describes a tale from their religious writings as a myth.

These modern Zoroastrians celebrate three thousand years of faith. Much like their ancient counterparts, they see myths as colorful tales that explain the origins and inner workings of their religion.

After Viraf visited hell, he returned with a very different tale. There, he recalled, he saw

> the soul of a man who [was endlessly] forced to [eat] dust and ashes. [And] I asked thus: "What sin was committed by this body, whose soul suffers such a punishment?" [An angel replied,] "This is the soul of that wicked man who, in the world, [was a merchant who cheated others]. I also saw the soul of a man who was held in the atmosphere, and fifty demons ever flogged him. . . . And I asked thus: "What sin was committed by this body, whose soul suffers such a punishment?" [The angel said,] "This is the soul of that wicked man who, in the world, was a bad ruler, and was unmerciful and destructive among men."[32]

The Renovation and First Savior

These and other similar mythical visions of heaven and hell were taken very seriously by everyday members of Persian society. Most people strongly believed that these places existed, and devout people did their best to live righteous lives, convinced this would ensure their entrance into heaven. At the same time, people were aware of other myths that told what would happen to humanity as a whole in the future. The common belief was that, being all-knowing, Ahura-Mazda was fully aware of what would transpire in the future. At some point, his visions of the future were revealed to humans, and these cosmic images were preserved in the form of myths.

The colorful Zoroastrian myths of the future collectively deal with a large-scale event called the Renovation. (That term also refers to the era in which the event will occur.) Here, that word means "restoration," in the sense of restoring the world to its original perfect state before the despicable Angra-Mainyu intruded and introduced evil, sorrow, and misery. In the Zoroastrian cosmic vision, the Renovation will take place in three grand stages, each lasting about one thousand years. At the end of each of these millennia, a savior will appear to help restore the world to a state of peace and goodness.

In the Zoroastrian myths the first thousand years of the Renovation are those directly following Zoroaster's life. Although modern historians think the prophet lived no later than 1000 B.C., most ancient sources held that he existed in the 600s B.C. Therefore the first savior, named Aushedar, should have appeared sometime around A.D. 400. (The fact that he did not appear as scheduled was explained by later Zoroastrian thinkers. They reorganized the original time periods spoken of in the myths to make the religious predictions better reflect the events of real life.)

In Persian myths Zoroaster, as shown here, educates and informs the people of the restoration of the world to its original perfect state before Angra-Mainyu introduced sorrow, evil, and misery into it.

In the myth of the first savior, Aushedar will be the off-spring of Zoroaster. This will be possible because the prophet's seed was long ago preserved in a lake. At the appropriate time, a fifteen-year-old virgin will bathe in the lake, and that special seed will enter her and cause Zoroaster's son to grow in her womb. He will be born, and when he reaches the age of thirty, the sun will stand still in the sky for ten days. At that point, the world will begin to improve, as increasing numbers of people accept the true religion of Ahura-Mazda and treat one another with respect and decency.

However, evil will still be present, and it will steadily manage to reassert itself. Eventually, a series of long, terrible winters will descend on the world and humanity. But some people and animals will survive inside the very same *vara* that Yima had constructed long ago. The *Denkard* speaks of

the perishing of most of mankind and animals within three winters and in the fourth, through the awfulness of those winters and the witchcraft of [an evil wizard named] Mahrkus. [And] during the fourth winter . . . the enclosure made by Yima [will open and from it will come the remnants of] mankind and animals and the [replenishing] of mankind and animals [will happen] again, arising specially from them.[33]

The Second and Third Saviors

As the human race begins to arise once more, the second savior—Aushedar-mah—will arrive to usher in the second thousand years of the Renovation. He will also be born of a virgin. In his myth,

when that man becomes thirty years old, the sun [will] stand still in the zenith of the sky for the duration of twenty days and nights, and it [will] shine over all the regions [of the world]. . . . [There will be] diminution of decay and extension of life, [and an] increase of humility and peace, and the perfection of liberality and enjoyment in the world. . . . On account of the freedom of mankind from wanting meat, they shall [give up] the eating of meat, and their food [will] become milk and vegetables. When three years have remained they shall [give up] even the drinking of milk, and their food and drink [will] become water and vegetables.[34]

The reference to future people becoming vegetarians might suggest to readers that the ancient Persians were vegetarian, but they were not. Herodotus, Xenophon (ZEN-uh-fon), and other ancient Greek writers witnessed Persians eating meat. However, some evidence suggests that most Persians consumed only small amounts of meat. K.E. Eduljee, a leading scholar of ancient Persia and the Zoroastrian faith, points out, "The Greek writings such as Xenophon's *Cyropaedia* [a biography of King Cyrus] leave us with the unmistakable impression that the Persians during the rule of Cyrus the Great were to be admired for their austerity and straightforwardness. The Persian diet was austere and the people were only occasional meat-eaters."[35]

Eduljee also says that even if most Persians sometimes ate meat, consuming a vegetarian diet may have been seen as an ideal goal or practice. Other historians suggest that the reference in this myth to future humans becoming vegetarians may have been added at some later point by a religious leader who rejected eating meat and wanted to promote vegetarianism among the faithful. Vegetarianism did indeed become an aspect of practicing Zoroastrianism. This shows how some elements of the Persian myths were added over time to reflect customs or ideas current in society.

The issue of meat-eating aside, the same myth claims that the age of the second savior will, like that of the first, end with a brief resurgence of evil. But soon afterward the third and final savior—Soshyant—will appear. Still another son of Zoroaster born of a virgin, this third rescuer of humanity will eliminate ills such as disease, misery, and death. In this way the final stage of the Renovation will be accomplished.

Soshyant's myth claims that he will also summon both the living and the souls of the dead and subject them to a last judgment. Any who are found to be wicked will be thrown down into hell for a short period and then purified in a fire (in some

The Existence of Suffering

Like people in all times and places, the Persians recognized that the world is full of suffering, and they wanted to know why that was so. Today, for instance, a common question posed in religious and philosophical discussions, especially in large-scale monotheistic faiths like Christianity and Judaism, is why God allows the existence of suffering. The answers vary widely from one religious denomination, leader, or thinker to another. When the ancient Persians asked this same question of their priests and leaders, however, they received a rather definitive answer. Namely, Ahura-Mazda did *not* allow suffering to exist. The precepts of the Persian faith and myths held that he was passion-ately opposed to suffering and other evils, which were caused by the evil one, Angra-Mainyu. Ahura-Mazda wanted to kill Angra-Mainyu and thereby rid the world of suffering. However, he could not do this immediately because that was not Ahura's destiny. Like the traditional Persian gods, he was not omnipotent, or all-powerful, so he could not choose to destroy evil sooner rather than later. However, Ahura-Mazda *was* omniscient, or all-knowing. As a result, he could see into the future, and there he saw that he, aided by his angels and untold numbers of righteous humans, would one day conquer and destroy evil altogether. Thus, eventually suffering would be eliminated completely.

versions a mass of white-hot molten metal). They will then be ready to enter heaven and join those who did not require punishment and purification. At that point the Amesha Spenta will go forth and destroy all the demons, and Ahura-Mazda himself will at last annihilate the evil one, Angra-Mainyu. In that triumphant moment, according to the *Denkard*,

> all the splendor, glory, and power, which have arisen in all those possessing splendor, glory, and power, are in him [Ahura-Mazda] on whom they arrive together and for those who are his, when many inferior human beings are aroused splendid and powerful. And through their power and glory all the troops of the fiend [Angra-Mainyu] are smitten [killed]. And all mankind [will thereafter] remain of one accord in the religion of Ahura-Mazda, owing to the will of the creator, the command of that apostle, and the resources of his companions.[36]

An expectant Zoroastrian mother is given sweets in her seventh month of pregnancy in the Zoroastrian Aghami ceremony. Many Zoroastrian holidays feature eating of sweets, nuts, and vegetables.

Character Shaped by Myths

It is important to emphasize that these myths of the future were viewed as prophecies of real historical events by followers of Zoroastrianism. An average person living in Sassanian Persia in the A.D. 300s, 400s, or 500s learned about these future events as a child. Thereafter, he or she likely accepted that they would happen someday, and that gave him or her a measure of confidence and peace of mind. After all, these and other Zoroastrian myths promoted certain "realties" that made Persia and its inhabitants seem special. First, the deity who had created humanity and still watched over it was Persian. Second, humanity's creation had taken place in Iran, and the Renovation to come would be centered there, too. Third, these "facts" implied that the Persian lands lay at the center of human civilization. So foreign peoples, like the Greeks, dwelled on the outer fringes of civilization and worshipped strange gods that, if real, were probably demons. Therefore, a Persian of the Sassanian Empire was fortunate, blessed, and inherently superior to any and all non-Persians. This was one of the ways that myths helped to shape the thinking and character of the inhabitants of ancient Iran.

CHAPTER 5

The Popular Legacy of Persian Myths

T he influence of ancient Persian religion and myths on later ages, peoples, and cultures has been multifaceted and far-reaching. Today Zoroastrianism itself is still practiced in some countries, and some of the old myths remain integral to the faith. Persian myths also survive and thrive in Persian literature, which remains popular in Iran and other parts of the Middle East. In addition, characters, events, and concepts from ancient Persian mythology have entered modern pop culture, not only in western Asia, but across the Western world as well. Storybooks, movies, graphic novels, and even video games have been based on the Persian myths. These serve to introduce some of the old tales, along with their gods, demons, kings, and heroes, to up-and-coming generations.

Survival of the Faith and Myths

The long-range charm, appeal, and staying power of the Persian myths was demonstrated by their repeated survival in ancient times. When the Greeks, led by Alexander the Great, conquered the Persian Empire in the fourth century B.C., the Zoroastrian faith, worship of the traditional Persian gods, and the myths accompanying both did not fade away. This was partly because the Greeks were tolerant of other peoples' faiths and did not demand that people in the conquered territories give up their traditional beliefs. But those old beliefs and myths remained viable also because they were deeply ingrained in a society that was already many centuries old.

Thereafter, Persian religion and myths survived several more centuries in the background of Greek and Parthian rule of large parts of the Middle East until the Sassanians carved out a new Persian Empire in the third century A.D. Sassanian rulers not only brought Zoroastrian religion back to the forefront of society, they also celebrated the old myths with colorful new retellings and added a number of new tales to the growing mythical storehouse. Persian religion became so popular in the Middle East during Sassanian times that it began to spread to neighboring regions. Evidence shows that at least by the late 400s, and possibly earlier, merchants and other travelers carried the faith into India and even as far away as northern China. Ruins of Zoroastrian fire temples have been found in the Chinese cities of Kaifeng and Zhenjiang.

The spread of Persian religion and myths stopped when the Arabs conquered Iran and neighboring lands in the 600s. However, once again the faith and its attendant tales survived. As in the case of the Greek conquests, this was partly due to tolerance among the invaders, for the Muslims did not impose their faith on the natives. However, over time various economic and social influences enticed large numbers of Persians to convert to Islam. So by the eleventh century, most of Iran and other Persian areas were predominantly Muslim. Nevertheless, a substantial minority of the population remained Zoroastrian, especially those who lived in outlying areas far from Baghdad, the Islamic cultural capital. Another factor that kept Persian beliefs and myths alive was the strong interest in them among Muslim intellectuals and writers, including Ferdowsi. His *Shahnameh* helped to cement the popularity of the

A Movie About Ferdowsi

A one-hour film titled *Ferdowsi* was made in 1934 about the life of that famous author of the *Shahnameh*. The director was the talented Iranian filmmaker Abdolhossein Sepanta, who also played the title role.

Some Surviving Myths About Alexander

In addition to the tales compiled in Ferdowsi's *Shahnameh* and other collections of myths from ancient and medieval Persia, several Persian myths about Alexander the Great survived into modern times. In one, Alexander's father, Philip, fell in love with a woman in his royal court, and she became pregnant. The king then asked his astrologers to examine the stars for any prophecies that might exist about the child to come. They answered that the child, a boy, would be uncommonly wise and would possess the key to controlling the whole world. The legend said that the grown Alexander would become a mighty military man, conquer Iran and India, and return to Greece with a Persian bride named Roxane. (In reality, he did not conquer India, died in Babylon at age thirty-two, and never made it back to Greece.)

In another, more humorous surviving myth, Alexander secretly had freakishly long ears, which he kept hidden beneath his golden crown. Only his personal slave knew the secret and was warned not to reveal it on pain of death. One day the slave could not keep the secret bottled up inside him any longer and screamed it into a well in the countryside. He did not realize that the secret was so profound that it escaped from the well and a country shepherd learned of it. Not long afterward, Alexander discovered that the secret was out and that his slave had been the culprit. But in the end he forgave the young man, for in his great wisdom Alexander realized that all secrets are eventually revealed.

After Alexander the Great (depicted in this bust) conquered the Persian Empire, many myths about him formed.

old Persian tales in Islamic culture for centuries to come and eventually in Western culture.

Unlike the case of the ancient Greek myths, which survived the disappearance of the original faith that produced them, Persian myths survived *along with* their religious beliefs.

Indeed, Zoroastrian religion is still practiced in India, the United States (which has the second-largest Zoroastrian community in the world), Iran, Canada, Australia, England, and other countries. The exact number of worshippers worldwide is unknown but is likely about two hundred thousand.

Also aiding the modern popularity of the Persian myths was a resurgence of interest in ancient Persian culture in Iran. The modern nation of Iran developed in the wake of World War I (1914–1918), when Reza Shah Pahlavi assumed leadership of the local residents. His son, Muhammad Reza Shah Pahlavi, became the country's leader, or shah, in 1941. Firmly backed by Western nations, including the United States, the shah launched major modernization programs. He also tried to boost Iranian patriotism by reviving interest in the original Persian Empire established by Cyrus II

This Zoroastrian fire temple held the sacred flame and is one of many in Iran. Zoroastrian fire temples were built as far away as northern China.

When Muhammad Reza Shah Pahlavi (pictured) became Iran's leader in 1941, he tried to boost Iranian patriotism by reviving interest in the ancient Persian Empire.

in the 500s B.C. In fact, the shah strongly identified himself as Cyrus's modern successor and encouraged his people to celebrate old Persian culture, including the stories and characters of the myths. New editions of Ferdowsi's *Shahnameh* were published, and storytellers and orators read the tales aloud in coffeehouses and parks.

In the 1970s, however, the shah was driven from Iran when a group of highly conservative Islamic leaders took charge of the country. Many Zoroastrians felt that the new regime was too restrictive of minority religions in Iran, including their own. So numerous followers of Zoroaster emigrated to other countries, including Canada and the United States. As a result, it is estimated that fewer than twenty thousand Zoroastrians remain in Iran today.

Customs Governed by Myths

No matter which country modern Zoroastrians make their home, their religious customs and rituals are the same. As in ancient times, they consist of set prayers, sacrifices, initiation ceremonies, and other practices, many of them guided by priests. Also as in past ages, most of the rituals are governed or inspired by highly respected myths.

Zoroastrian funerary rites constitute a clear example of this relationship between ancient myths and modern rituals. Among the best-known ancient myths are those involving the Zoroastrian devil, Angra-Mainyu, and his attempts to corrupt humanity. These stories make it clear that disease and death are part of the devil's corruptive influence. One important result of this fact, as the myths instruct the faithful, is that directly following death, a human corpse is inhabited by demons or other evil forces. So the body must be purified, or cleansed, of such evil before it can undergo its last rites.

The specific ways to handle a dead body, to purify it, and to perform the funeral are also explained in brief myths that appear as discussions between Zoroaster and Ahura-Mazda in the *Avesta*. In a passage in the *Vendidad*, for instance, the prophet asks what mourners should do with the body after it has been cleansed and prepared, and God answers,

> They shall let the lifeless body lie [in a special room or else in a specially dug hole in the ground filled with stone or sand] for two nights, or three nights, or a month long, until the birds begin to fly. . . . Then the worshippers of Mazda shall make a breach in the wall of the house, and two men, strong and skillful [that is, specially trained for the job], having stripped their clothes off [and put on special clothes], shall take up the body from the [ground] or from the plastered house, and they shall lay it down on a place where they know there are always corpse-eating . . . birds.[37]

It is known that the ancient Persians practiced the customs mentioned in this myth because Herodotus described them in his famous history book. Devout Zoroastrians still follow them either exactly or fairly closely. After a corpse has been washed carefully, professional corpse handlers, always two in number, as in the myth, make sure that it lies either in a room in a house or in a specially prepared place outside. Only those two individuals touch the body, because it is thought that if ordinary people touch it they may be corrupted by evil. (The handlers themselves are periodically purified in a ceremony designed to rid them of any evil they may have come into contact with in their work.)

Throughout the night before the funeral, family, friends, and a priest say prayers. Then, in the morning, a funeral procession forms with everyone, beginning with the corpse handlers, marching in groups of two. They take the body to a place where vultures—the "corpse-eating birds" mentioned by God in the myth—will consume the flesh. (In a few places in the world where this use of vultures is impossible or not allowed, cremation has been adopted as an alternative.)

Herodotus on Persian Burials

Herodotus, the fifth-century-B.C. Greek historian, said the following about Persian burial customs, some of which Zoroastrians still observe and some of which they do not:

There is another practice . . . concerning the burial of the dead, which is not spoken of openly and is something of a mystery. It is that a male Persian is never buried until the body has been torn by a bird. I know for certain that the Magi [Persian priests] have this custom, for they are quite open about it. The Persians in general, however, cover a body with wax and then bury it. The Magi are a peculiar caste, quite different from the Egyptian priests and indeed from any other sort of person. [They] not only kill anything, except dogs and men, with their own hands, but make a special point of doing so. Ants, snakes . . . birds—no matter what—they kill them indiscriminately. Well, it is an ancient custom, so let them keep it!

Herodotus. *The Histories.* Translated by Aubrey de Sélincourt. New York: Penguin, 2003, pp. 98–99.

Binding Oneself to God

Young Iranians perform the navjote *ceremony, or rite of initiation into the Zoroastrian community. It is the most important event in a child's life.*

Another important Zoroastrian ritual inspired and informed by cherished myths is the *navjote*, the ceremony of initiation, in which a young person pledges his or her life and soul to God. In so doing, the person also rejects Angra-Mainyu and the evils associated with that devil-like figure. Thus, the ritual of initiation is based in part on the original Zoroastrian myth of the ongoing battle between God and evil. It is also based on the myths that describe the judgment of the soul after death and the final judgment that will be performed by the third savior in the future. By officially joining the faith in the initiation ceremony, a person is agreeing to be judged in the manner depicted in those myths.

The ceremony itself begins with a priest and his assistants sitting opposite to and facing the initiate on the floor or a raised platform. According to a prominent member of the faith, "One of the assistants maintains the fire, called the Atash Dadgah. The initiate sits on a low stool, called a patlo, covered with a white sheet. Most Zoroastrian ceremonies are conducted on the floor [to remind people] to be humble, to be grounded, and to stay connected with the earth and nature."[38]

The initiate starts by repenting his or her past sins, after which prayers are said. Next the priest wraps a hollow, knotted cord around the initiate's waist to symbolize the binding commitment being made to the faith. The initiate then recites the Fravarane, a solemn pledge to abide by God's rules and live a good, upright life. Part of the pledge states, "I am a worshipper of God, a Zoroastrian in worship of God. These pledges and intents I do declare. I pledge my thoughts to good thoughts. I pledge my speech to good words. I pledge my actions to good deeds. I pledge myself to the highest discerning belief in worship of God."[39]

Through these and other religious rituals, several of the Persian myths continue to have significant meaning today, thousands of years after they first appeared. This is possible because of the remarkable diligence of members of the faith in each new generation. During those long centuries, they carefully preserved and passed along the myths, partly in written form and partly by word of mouth.

The Myths in Popular Media

Another way that some of the old Persian myths are being preserved in the modern world is through the popular media. These include graphic novels, movies, and video games, of which the graphic novels are the most faithful in reproducing the characters, events, and cultural settings of the original stories. The most outstanding example yet is a series of graphic novels produced by Bruce Bahmani. An American of Iranian descent, he spent several of his childhood years in Iran and there became closely familiar with Persian culture. Particularly fascinating and thrilling for him

Rustam the Trickster

In the *Shahnameh*, Rustam is often called Rustam-e-Dastan, meaning "Rustam the trickster." This is what gave the makers of the movie *Prince of Persia* the idea to name the main character Prince Dastan.

were the rousing tales of Zal, Rustam, and other swashbuckling heroes who appear in Ferdowsi's classic *Shahnameh*.

As an adult, Bahmani felt that translating some of these tales into the graphic novel format would be an effective way to take the old Persian myths beyond Iran to a wider international public. Working with gifted artist Karl Altstaetter, he created the series *Rostam: Tales from the Shahnameh*, which has received glowing reviews. Iranian-born journalist and film historian Darius Kadivar says that these colorful renderings of Ferdowsi's classic offer a "modern look [at] its heroes while respecting the historical accuracies in respect to the costumes and sets. The result is a journey through Persian mythology that reminds me very much of Peter Jackson's faithful film adaptation of J.R.R. Tolkien's *Lord of the Rings*, shot and produced in New Zealand."[40]

While Bahmani has tried to maintain a fair level of accuracy and faithfulness to the original myths, some of the other popular media versions of these tales have not. An example is the video game *Garshasp: The Monster Slayer*, released in 2011. It is a very loose adaptation of the mythical adventures of the Persian hero Keresaspa, who slew numerous monsters and evil beings. He also appears in the myths about the future, in which, it is said, Ahura-Mazda will resurrect him and assign him the task of killing the evil demon Azhi Dahaka. The story in the *Garshasp* game does deal with the hero's confrontation with Azhi Dahaka, but many of the events, locales, and characters are modern fabrications that do not appear in the original.

A series of video games released between 1989 and 2008 under the general title *Prince of Persia* takes even more liberties with the original myths. Among the games are *Prince of Persia: The Warrior Within* and *Prince of Persia: The Sands of Time*, released in 2003. The latter was made into a live-action movie by Walt Disney Pictures and released in 2010. The film, directed by Mike Newell, stars Jake Gyllenhaal in the lead role of Prince Dastan. That

Becoming a Responsible Person

In his extensive writings about his faith, modern Zoroastrian K.E. Eduljee explains some of the reasoning behind the Zoroastrian initiation ceremony, the navjote, *including how the age of the initiate has changed over time.*

At birth, an individual is born into the care of her or his parents and remains their ward until the coming of age. After a *navjote*, the person is born again into a new life, this time as a responsible person, accountable in this life and the after-life for every thought, word and deed. . . . Perhaps we can take this to mean that the responsibility for a person's thoughts, words and deeds now resides within that person, within their soul. During the *navjote* ceremony, the initiate makes a pledge to abide by the [tenets] of the faith, a covenant that a Zoroastrian will renew every time she or he recites [his or her] prayers. The initiate should therefore have the capacity to enter into this pledge, to maintain the pledge, and to be responsible and accountable for every thought, word and deed. In Mithraic terms (Mithra is the angel and guardian of contracts and

promises), the pledge is a binding contract containing covenants. At some time after the Arab invasion of Iran . . . the age for the initiation ceremony was lowered and a child could be initiated after the age of seven. Nowadays, for children born to Zoroastrian parents, the *navjote* ceremony takes place between the ages of seven and twelve.

K.E. Eduljee. "Initiation into the Zoroastrian Faith." Zoroastrian Heritage. http://heritageinstitute.com/zoroastrianism/navjote/index.htm.

During the navjote *ceremony the initiate makes a pledge to be responsible and accountable for every thought, word, and deed.*

Between 1989 and 2008 several games based on Persian myths were released under the Prince of Persia *title, one of which is shown here. One game was also made into a movie.*

character, along with the plot, are said to be inspired by the heroes from the Persian myths, but the filmmakers did not attempt to portray the actual characters or to follow the actual events of those stories. Instead, the plot revolves around a magical dagger that can reverse the flow of time and the attempts by some evil characters to exploit it. Nevertheless, the movie does manage to capture the magical, larger-than-life atmosphere of the myths and thereby has helped to popularize them among a number of action hero fans around the world.

Reduced to Tears

In spite of the advent of electronic media like radio, television, movies, video games, and the Internet, the old Persian myths have survived in no less a dramatic fashion by simple word of mouth. During medieval times professional storytellers known as *naqqal* flourished in the Middle East, especially in Iran. They put on little shows on street corners, in marketplaces, and/or wherever they could gather a local crowd. Employing colorful costumes, props such as swords and clubs, and painted backdrops to set the scene, they recited, sang, and acted out the tales told in the ancient myths. Most often requested and performed were the stories of Rustam and the other heroes from Ferdowsi's *Shahnameh*.

An Iranian storyteller, or naqqal, sings a tale from Persian mythology. The practice of professional storytellers is a tradition going back to medieval times.

The *naqqal* still perform in Iran and some neighboring lands today. People of all ages, but particularly youngsters, avidly watch the performances and cheer when a hero vanquishes a demon or monster. As scholar Vesta S. Curtis describes it:

> Through gesticulation [broad hand gestures] and a combination of poetry recitation and singing, the *naqqal* carries his listeners with him from battlefield to royal court, making them laugh with his mimicry [role-playing] and reducing them to tears with moving descriptions of poignant and brutal murders. These stories are often interrupted at crucial points and continued the following day, thus stretching one story over several days.[41]

Thanks to these shows, poorer folk who have little or no access to electronic media learn about some important aspects of their cultural heritage. This was how their ancestors learned about ancient Persia's surviving myths. In all likelihood, many future generations of people in the region will absorb them that way, too. If that is the case, these fabulous tales may well end up being as immortal as some of the characters they describe.

NOTES

Introduction: Why Persian Myths Remain Relevant

1. John R. Hinnells. *Persian Mythology*. North Palm Beach, FL: Chancellor, 1997, pp. 7–8.

Chapter 1: Myth and History Intertwined: Persian Origins

2. Hinnells. *Persian Mythology*, p. 117.
3. Hinnells. *Persian Mythology*, p. 22.
4. Michael Kerrigan. "Legends of the Early World." In *Wise Lord of the Sky: Persian Myth*, edited by Tony Allan et al. London: Time-Life, 1999, pp. 28–29.
5. Herodotus. *The Histories*. Translated by Aubrey de Sélincourt. New York: Penguin, 2003, p. 86.
6. Herodotus. *The Histories*, p. 556.
7. Charles Phillips. "The Persian World." In Allan et al. *Wise Lord of the Sky*, p. 13.
8. Quoted in Hinnells. *Persian Mythology*, p. 32.
9. Tony Allan. "Land of the Story-Tellers." In Allan et al., *Wise Lord of the Sky*, pp. 112–113.
10. Quoted in Alessandro Bausani. *The Persians: From the Earliest Days to the Twentieth Century*. Translated by J.B. Donne. London: Elek, 1975, p. 27.
11. Herodotus. *The Histories*, p. 98.
12. Phillips. "The Persian World," pp. 20–23.

Chapter 2: The Early Gods: Society's Protectors

13. Hinnells. *Persian Mythology*, p. 27.
14. *Hymn to Tishtrya. Khorda Avesta*. Translated by James Darmesteter. Avesta—Zoroastrian Archives. www.avesta.org/ka/yt8sbe.htm.
15. *Hymn to Tishtrya*.
16. *Hymn to the Waters, Khorda Avesta*. Translated by James Darmesteter. Avesta—Zoroastrian Archives. www.avesta.org/ka/yt5sbe.htm.
17. *Hymn to the Waters*.
18. *Hymn to the Waters*.
19. Herodotus. *The Histories*, p. 103.
20. *Hymn to Verethragna, Khorda Avesta*. Translated by James Darmesteter. Avesta—Zoroastrian Archives. www.avesta.org/ka/yt14sbe.htm.
21. Kerrigan. "Legends of the Early World," p. 33.
22. *Hymn to Mithra, Khorda Avesta*. Translated by James Darmesteter. Avesta—Zoroastrian Archives. www.avesta.org/ka/yt10sbe.htm.

Chapter 3: Persia's Mythical Kings and Heroes

23. Kerrigan. "Legends of the Early World," p. 39.
24. Quoted in A. Berriedale Keith and Albert J. Carnoy. *The Mythology of All Races, Volume VI: Indian and Iranian*. New York: Cooper Square, 1964, p. 310.
25. Phillips. "The Persian World," p. 63.
26. Hinnells. *Persian Mythology*, pp. 103, 108.
27. *Vendidad, Fargard 2*. Translated by James Darmesteter. Avesta—Zoroastrian Archives. www.avesta.org/vendidad/vd2sbe.htm.
28. Norma L. Goodrich. *Ancient Myths*. New York: New American Library, 1960, pp. 133–134.

Chapter 4: The Myths and Realities of Zoroaster

29. *Denkard, Book 7*. Translated by E.W. West. Avesta—Zoroastrian Archives. www.avesta.org/denkard/dk7.html.
30. *Denkard, Book 7*.
31. *Book of Arda Viraf*. Translated by Martin Haug. Avesta—Zoroastrian Archives. www.avesta.org/mp/viraf.html.
32. *Book of Arda Viraf*.
33. *Denkard, Book 7*.
34. *Denkard, Book 7*.
35. K.E. Eduljee. "Achaemenian Persian King's Table." Zoroastrian Heritage, June 22, 2011. http://zoroastrianheritage.blogspot.com/2011/07/achaemenian-persian-kings-table.html.
36. *Denkard, Book 7*.

Chapter 5: The Popular Legacy of Persian Myths

37. *Vendidad, Book 8*. Translated by James Darmesteter. Avesta—Zoroastrian Archives. www.avesta.org/vendidad/vd8sbe.htm.
38. K.E. Eduljee. "Initiation into the Zoroastrian Faith." Zoroastrian Heritage. http://heritageinstitute.com/zoroastrianism/navjote/index.htm.
39. Quoted in Eduljee. "Initiation into the Zoroastrian Faith."
40. Darius Kadivar. "Rostam Super Hero: Popularizing a Persian Myth." www.theshahnameh.com/page/rostam-super-hero-popularizing.
41. Vesta S. Curtis. *Persian Myths*. Austin: University of Texas Press, 1993, p. 77.

GLOSSARY

Asa: In the Zoroastrian faith, the truth, that is, the great honesty and goodness of God (Ahura-Mazda) and his followers.

daevas: Early Iranian gods; in the Zoroastrian faith they are often viewed as evil demons and spirits.

Divine Glory: The god-given authority for a Persian king to rule his people and empire; also, a radiant glow surrounding a worthy king.

Drug: In the Zoroastrian faith, the lie, that is, the great deceit and evil associated with Angra-Mainyu and his wicked followers.

dynasty: A family line of rulers.

farohar: A symbol of kingly and/or divine authority that appeared above most ancient Persian carvings and inscriptions.

farr: The Persian word for Divine Glory (see above).

Fravarane: A religious pledge made by a Zoroastrian during his or her initiation into the faith.

inscription: One or more words carved into a durable material, such as stone or metal.

magi: Priests of the Zoroastrian religion.

monotheist: Someone who worships a single god.

naqqal: Iranian storytellers who recite and perform old Persian myths on street corners and in other public places.

navjote: The initiation ceremony in which a Zoroastrian enters the faith.

orthodox: In the religious sense, strict and conservative.

pantheon: A group of gods worshipped by a people.

polytheist: Someone who worships multiple gods.

proskenysis: A Greek word denoting the ancient Persian custom of lying prostrate, or facedown on the floor or ground, before a ruler or social superior.

prototype: The model for or first important example of something or someone.

Renovation: In the Zoroastrian faith, the large-scale and far-reaching restoration of order and goodness to the world and humanity that God will bring about in the future.

sacrifice: An offering made to appease a god or gods.

stelae: Stone or wooden slabs often used as boundary markers.

vara: In various Persian myths, a large enclosure built to keep out the winter cold and preserve the lives of people and animals inside.

Yasht: Hymns to various gods contained in the Zoroastrian holy book the *Avesta*.

Yazatas: Heavenly spirits or minor angels.

Books

Tony Allan et al. *Wise Lord of the Sky: Persian Myth*. London: Time-Life, 1999. A well-written, informative, nicely illustrated volume that provides plenty of background information about Persian history while describing many of the better-known Persian myths.

Mary Boyce. *Zoroastrians: Their Religious Beliefs and Practices*. Boston: Routledge and Kegan Paul, 2001. This is a solid introduction to the Zoroastrian faith and its rituals, which are intricately bound up in myths.

J.M. Cook. *The Persians*. London: Folio Society, 2002. One of the leading modern experts on ancient Persia gives a good general overview of ancient Persian history and society.

John Curtis. *Ancient Persia*. London: British Museum Press, 2011. A short, easy-to-read, but informative volume summarizing Persian history, ethnicity, art, and architecture.

John Curtis and St. John Simpson. *The World of Achaemenid Persia: The Diversity of Iran*. London: I.B. Tauris, 2010. This well-written, easy-to-read volume tells how the Persian Empire developed and describes what few aspects of Persian life are known.

Vesta S. Curtis. *Persian Myths*. Austin: University of Texas Press, 1993. This is a brief but well-written and authoritative synopsis and analysis of the characters and themes of Persian/ Iranian mythology.

Ferdowsi. *The Shahnameh: The Persian Book of Kings*. Translated by Dick Davis. New York: Penguin, 2007. An easy-to-read translation of Ferdowsi's delightful collection of Persian myths, thought to have been written in the late A.D. 900s.

John R. Hinnells. *Persian Mythology*. North Palm Beach, FL: Chancellor, 1997. Hinnells, a Manchester University scholar, presents a comprehensive, enlightening summary of ancient Persian mythology, devoting the bulk of his discussion to Zoroastrian characters and stories (which incorporated characters and themes from older Iranian myths).

Harold Lamb. *Cyrus the Great*. Wellington, New Zealand: Pinnacle, 1976. This excellent modern telling of the life, times, and myths of Cyrus, founder of the Persian Empire, is still popular and very worthwhile for both high school students and older readers.

Don Nardo. *Ancient Persia*. San Diego: Thomson Gale, 2003. Aimed at juvenile readers, this colorfully illustrated volume summarizes the main points of ancient Persian history and religion and cites several passages from Herodotus's comments about Persia.

Virginia Schomp. *Myths of the World: The Ancient Persians*. Tarrytown, NY: Marshall Cavendish, 2010. This very worthwhile collection of major Persian myths was written for junior high and high school students but will appeal to adults as well.

Websites

Avesta—Zoroasrtian Archives (www.avesta.org/avesta.html). This is a central hub that lists dozens of links to English translations of the *Avesta* and other Zoroastrian sacred writings, along with all sorts of fascinating related material.

Ferdowsi's Shahnameh, Zoroastrian Heritage (http://heritageinstitute.com/zoroastrianism/shahnameh/index.htm). This is an excellent introduction to Ferdowsi's epic collection of Persian myths, with much helpful information about the poet and the background of the work itself.

Greek Perceptions of Zoroaster, Zoroastrianism, and the Magi (http://zoroastrianheritage.blogspot.com/2011/04/greek-perceptions-of-zoroaster.html). This useful site summarizes the major ancient Greek writers who described the Persians and their myths and includes some interesting quotes by them.

Heroes—Their Story in Brief, Zoroastrian Heritage (http://heritageinstitute.com/zoroastrianism/shahnameh/heros.htm). This site nicely summarizes the exploits of the main mythical Persian heroes, including Zal and Rustam.

Persians. Kidipede (www.historyforkids.org/learn/westasia/history/persians.htm). This worthwhile site has a brief summary of Persian history, supplemented by several color photos of Persian ruins and several links to related topics.

INDEX

PICTURE CREDITS

Cover: © M. Khebra/ShutterStock.com

© 19th era 2/Alamy, 53

© Abedin Taherkenareh/epa/Corbis, 70

© The Art Archive at Art Resource, NY, 23, 65, 72

© Bibliothèque des Arts Decoratifs, Paris, France/Archives Charmet/ The Bridgeman Art Library, 29, 67

© Bibliothèque Nationale, Paris, France/The Bridgeman Art Library, 38

© The Bridgeman Art Library, 41

© Business Wire via Getty Images, 88

©Czartoryski Museum, Cracow, Poland/The Bridgeman Art Library, 60

© Earl & Nazima Kowall/Corbis, 89

© Erich Lessing/Art Resource, NY, 17, 51

© Fox Photos/Getty Images, 81

Gale/Cengage Learning, 4, 5, 6–7

© Gianni Dagli Orti/The Art Archive at Art Resource, NY, 56, 80

© Giraudon/The Bridgeman Art Library, 21

© HIP/Art Resource, NY, 19

© The Israel Museum/The Bridgeman Art Library, 32

© J. Baylor Roberts/National Geographic/Getty Images, 14

© Kaveh Kazemi/Getty Images, 34, 63

© Lindsay Hebberd/Corbis, 84

© Look and Learn/The Bridgeman Art Library, 27

© NGS Image Collection/The Art Archive at Art Resource, NY, 59

© Roger Cracknell 01/classic/Alamy, 79

© Scala/Art Resource, NY, 43, 45

© SEF/Art Resource, NY, 10, 16, 48

© Tim Page/Corbis, 76, 87

ABOUT THE AUTHOR

Historian Don Nardo has written numerous acclaimed volumes about ancient civilizations and peoples. Among these are studies of the religious beliefs and myths of those peoples, including the Greeks, Romans, Egyptians, Sumerians, and others. Nardo also composes and arranges orchestral music. He resides with his wife, Christine, in Massachusetts.